THE WORLD'S GREATEST AIRCRAFT

EARLY FIGHTERS

THE WORLD'S GREATEST AIRCRAFT
EARLY FIGHTERS

Christopher Chant: edited by Michael J.H. Taylor

Chelsea House Publishers • Philadelphia

Published in 2000 by
Chelsea House Publishers
1974 Sproul Road, Suite 400
P.O. Box 914
Broomall. PA, 19008-0914

ISBN 0-7910-5418-7

Copyright © 2000 Regency House Publishing Limited

Photographs on pages 2, 3, 6–7, 8-9 courtesy © Austin J.
Brown Aviation Picture Library

Printed in China

Library of Congress Cataloging-in-Publication Data

Chant, Christopher.
    Early Fighters / by Christopher Chant.
        p.   cm. -- (The world's greatest aircraft)
    Originally published as part of the author's: The
world's greatest aircraft. London: Grange Books, 1997.
    Includes index.
    Summary: Drawings, photographs, and text describe a
variety of fighter planes, both U.S. and foreign, in use in
World Wars I and II, including Britain's Sopwith Camel, the
German Fokker and Messerschmitts, the American Curtiss
series and the Lockheed Lightning.
    ISBN 0-7910-5418-7
    1. Fighter planes Juvenile literature. [1. Fighter planes.
2. Airplanes, Military.] I. Title. II. Series.
UG1242.F5C416 1999
623.7'464--do21   99-30765
                                                          CIP

Page 2: Fokker Triplane
Page 3: Fokker DR1
Right: Boeing F4B-4
Frontispiece: Supermarine Spitfire MK.16E
Contents pages: Hawker Hurricane

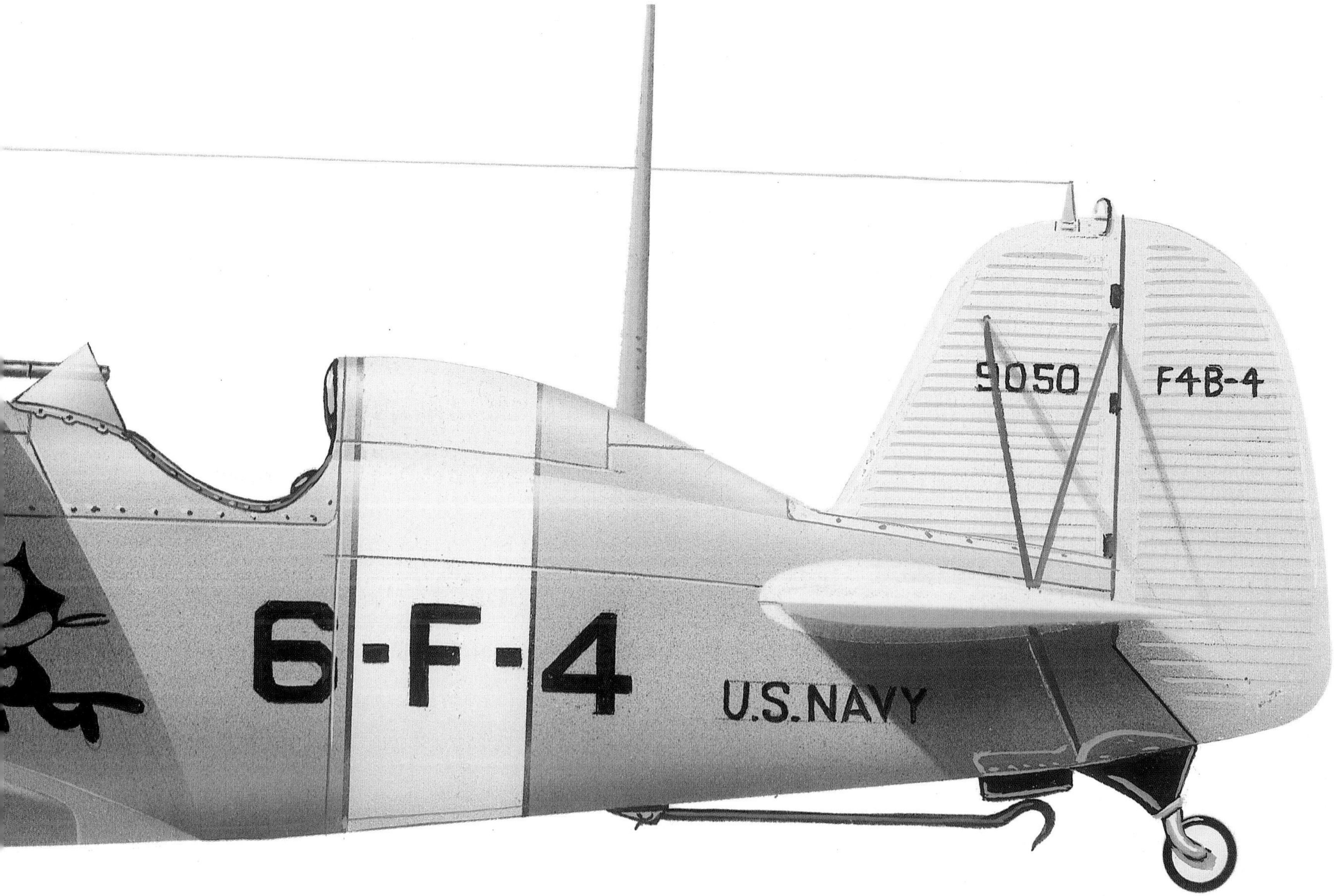
9050
F4B-4
6-F-4
U.S.NAVY

Piston-Engined Fighters

Tremendous pioneering achievements in the field of aeroplane development during the first decade of the 20th century meant that it took under six years from the first flight of the Wright *Flyer* to put a military aeroplane into service with the U.S. Army, in the form of a Wright Model A in 1909. Just two years later, reconnaissance and light bombing using aeroplanes had been extensively practised within America and by others abroad, and in the same year Italy flew the world's first operational missions against Turkish forces, observing positions and dropping explosives. With land warfare conducted by vast ground armies, aeroplanes were seen as convenient 'eyes in the sky', of greater worth than tethered observation balloons but not so vital that they should be allowed to *frighten the horses*.

Meanwhile, in 1910 a rifle had been fired from a U.S. Army Curtiss biplane. Little significance was drawn from the event and no immediate thought was given to the possibility of arming aeroplanes with guns. Reconnaissance, light bombing and artillery spotting, therefore, continued to be the official roles for aeroplanes up to and beyond the outbreak of World War I. Similarly, when in Britain in 1911 Major Brooke-Popham of the Air Battalion, Royal Engineers, attempted to fix a gun to a Blériot monoplane, he was ordered to remove it in no uncertain terms. Apathy also attended experiments in America in June 1912, when the newly-invented Lewis machine-gun was fired from an Army Signal Corps Wright Model B by Captain Charles de Forest Chandler. However, the day of the fighting aeroplane was drawing close.

The British Admiralty became an early driving force for arming offensive aeroplanes, and in November 1912 contracted Vickers to design and produce an experimental fighting biplane. The Vickers EFB1 Destroyer, as it became, was put on display at the February 1913 Olympia Aero Show, featuring a rear-mounted pusher engine/propeller and a nose-mounted Vickers-Maxim machine-gun with a 60° angle of vertical/horizontal movement. Also appearing

at the Show was Claude Grahame-White's Type 6 Military Biplane, which offered a wider field of fire for its Colt gun. It was, however, the Destroyer that is best remembered, leading eventually to the development of the famed wartime FB5 Gun Bus fighter which joined British forces in France in early 1915.

Both British fighters at Olympia in 1913 featured pusher engines and propellers, allowing the nose gun in each to be fired forwards without the worry of hitting the propeller. Other countries later adopted combat aircraft of similar layout, notably the French Voisin that, in early form in October 1914, claimed the first-ever air-to-air victory by gunfire, shooting down a German two-seater.

Since 1913 several countries had produced 'scouting' aeroplanes, front-engined biplanes and monoplanes of more modern streamlined design than the pusher types, often single-seaters and intended mainly for high-speed unarmed reconnaissance but also capable of other uses including 'nuisance' raids and light bombing. Because of their front-turning propellers, fitting them with forward-firing guns had not appeared possible. But, if this could be done, a deadly new weapon would emerge, capable of catching and destroying enemy reconnaissance aircraft and even scouts before they reported back to base. The problem to be faced, however, looked daunting; how to fire a machine-gun through the arc of a turning propeller without damaging the blades and thereby destroying the aircraft.

Raymond Saulnier of the Morane-Saulnier company in France and Franz Schneider of LVG in Germany worked separately on the problem and in 1913/14 devised systems, but for various technical reasons neither was adopted. Instead, with war declared, Morane-Saulnier came up with a simple alternative and fitted deflector plates (wedges to divert striking bullets) to the propeller of a Morane-Saulnier monoplane, providing a solution of sorts without technical diffficulty. Given an early machine, Frenchman Roland Garros shot down his first enemy aircraft on April 1 1915, the first-ever air victory by a fighter firing a gun through the propeller arc.

Unfortunately, he made an emergency landing behind enemy lines on the 19th, thereby passing the secret to the Germans.

Though Germany viewed the deflector system with interest, Fokker returned to the better synchronized 'interrupter' gear method of timing bullets to fire between the turning blades and quickly convinced the authorities that he had a workable system. First combat tested on a converted Fokker M5K reconnaissance monoplane with great success, it lead to the production of the world's first operational

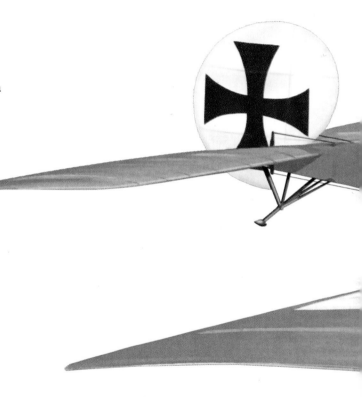

fighter with a synchronized gun, the single-seat Fokker E series Eindecker. Though not fast, the small number of Eindeckers soon widened their role from merely offering defence for German reconnaissance two-seaters to searching the skies for vulnerable Allied aircraft. For ten months from the summer of 1915 Eindeckers dominated the Western Front, a period that became known to the Allies as the 'Fokker Scourge' due to extremely heavy losses. The true fighter had exploded onto the scene.

Picture: Fokker E.III, the improved and most produced version of the famous Eindecker fighter of the First World War.

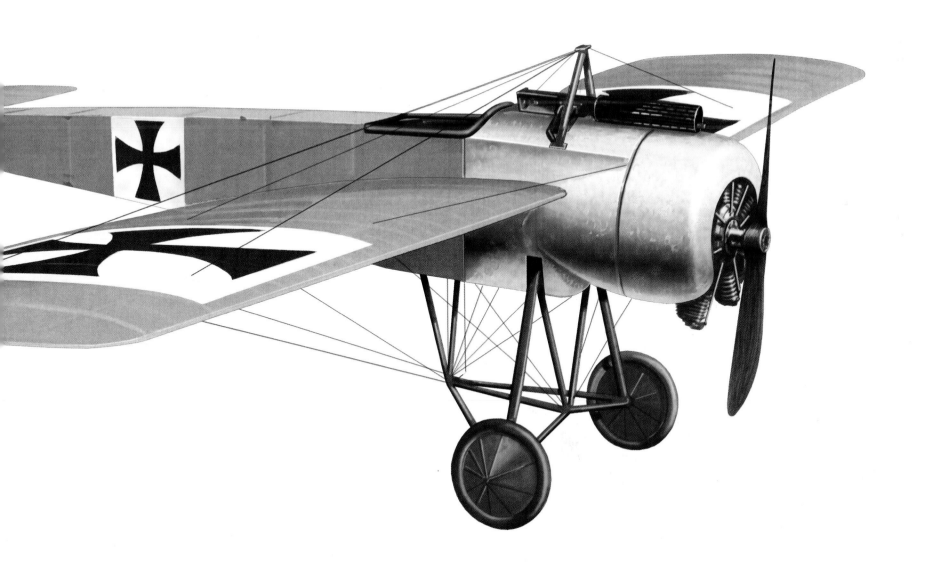

NIEUPORT 11 BEBE and 17 (France)

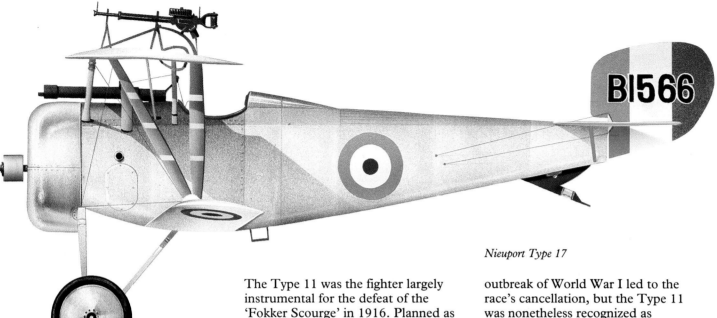

BI566

Nieuport Type 17

The Type 11 was the fighter largely instrumental for the defeat of the 'Fokker Scourge' in 1916. Planned as a competition sesquiplane to take part in the Gordon Bennett Trophy race of 1914, the first Type 11 was designed and built in a mere four months. The outbreak of World War I led to the race's cancellation, but the Type 11 was nonetheless recognized as possessing the performance and flight characteristics to make it a useful military aircraft. Early Type 11 aircraft were powered by the 60-kW (80-hp) Le Rhône rotary engine, and were used by the French and British as scouts from 1915. The aircraft's apparent daintiness led to the nickname Bébé (Baby). The Type 11 was then turned into a fighter by the addition of a machine-gun on the upper-wing centre section to fire over the propeller's swept disc.

Many more aircraft were built under licence in Italy by Macchi with the designation Nieuport 1100. The Type 16 was a version with the 82-kW (110-hp) Le Rhône rotary for better performance. The Type 17 was a further expansion of the same design concept with a strengthened airframe but the same 82-kW (110-hp) Le Rhône. The new model retained its predecessors' excellent agility but offered superior performance, including a sparkling rate of climb. The fighter's 7.7-mm (0.303-in) Lewis gun was located on a sliding mount that allowed the pilot to pull the weapon's rear down, allowing oblique upward fire and also making for easier reloading.

The slightly later Type 17bis introduced the 97-kW (130-hp) Clerget rotary and a synchronized machine-gun on the upper fuselage. Still later models were the Type 21 with the 60-kW (80 hp), later the 82-kW (110 hp), Le Rhône and larger ailerons, and the slightly heavier Type 23 with 60- or 89-kW (120 hp) Le Rhône engines.

Nieuport 11.

NIEUPORT TYPE 11
Role: Fighter
Crew/Accommodation: One
Power Plant: One 80 hp Gnome or Le Rhône 9C air-cooled rotary
Dimensions: Span 7.55 m (24.77 ft); length 5.8 m (19.03 ft); wing area 13 m² (140 sq ft)
Weights: Empty 344 kg (759 lb); MTOW 550 kg (1,213 lb)
Performance: Maximum speed 156 km/h (97 mph) at sea level; operational ceiling 4,600 m (15,090 ft); range 330 km (205 miles) with full bombload
Load: One .303 inch machine gun

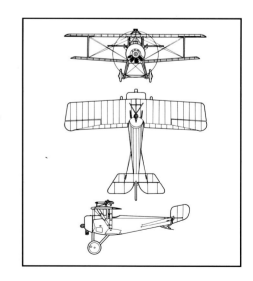

Nieuport Type 11 Bébé

SPAD S.7 AND S.13 (France)

SPAD S.13

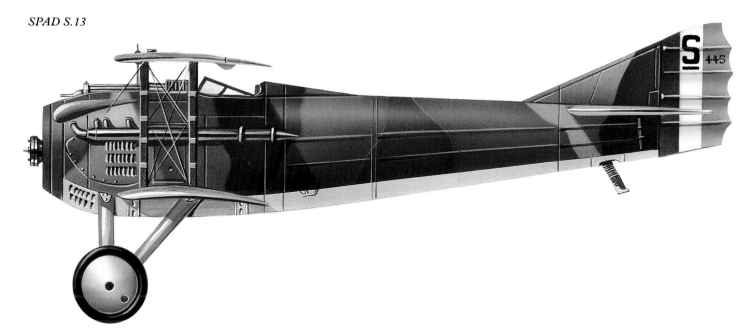

Vickers machine-gun, and was a sturdy two-bay biplane with unstaggered wings, fixed tailskid landing gear, and a wooden structure covered with fabric except over the forward fuselage, which was skinned in light alloy. Delivery of the essentially similar first production series of about 500 aircraft began in September 1916, being followed by some 6,000 examples of an improved model with the 134-kW (180-hp) HS 8Ac engine and wings of slightly increased span. In 1917 the company flew two development aircraft, and the S.12 with the 149-kW (200-hp) HS 8Bc paved the way for a production series of some 300 aircraft including some with the 164-kW (220-hp) HS 8Bec engine between the cylinder banks of which nestled a 37-mm *moteur canon*. Further development produced the S.13 that first flew in April 1917 for service from May of the same year. This has two guns rather than one, more power, slightly greater span and a number of aerodynamic refinements. Production of this superb fighter totalled 8,472 aircraft.

These two closely related aircraft were France's best fighters of World War I, combining high performance and structural strength without too great a sacrifice of agility. The result was an excellent gun platform comparable with the S.E.5a in British service. After experience with the A1 to A5 aircraft, designer Louis Béchereau turned to the conventional tractor biplane layout for the S.5 that first flew in the closing stages of 1915 and became in effect the prototype for the S.7, which was the first genuinely successful warplane developed by the Société Pour 1'Avions et ses Dérives which is what the original but bankrupt Société Pour les Appareils Deperdussin became after its purchase by Louis Blériot.

The first S.7 flew early in 1916 with a 112-kW (150-hp) Hispano-Suiza 8Aa inline and a single synchronized 7.7-mm (0.303-in)

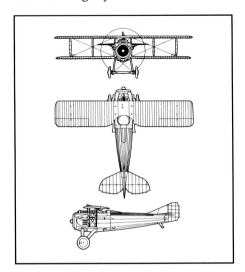

SPAD S.7

SPAD S.13
Role: Fighter
Crew/Accommodation: One
Power Plant: One 220 hp Hispano-Suiza 8BEC water-cooled inline
Dimensions: Span 8 m (26.3 ft); length 6.2 m (20.33 ft); wing area 21.1 m² (227.1 sq ft)
Weights: Empty 565 kg (1,245 lb); MTOW 820 kg (1,807 lb)
Performance: Maximum speed 222 km/h (138 mph) at sea level; operational ceiling 5,400 m (17,717 ft); range 402 km (250 miles)
Load: Two .303 inch machine guns

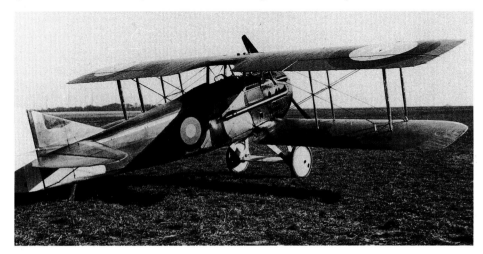

SPAD S.13

ALBATROS D III and D V (Germany)

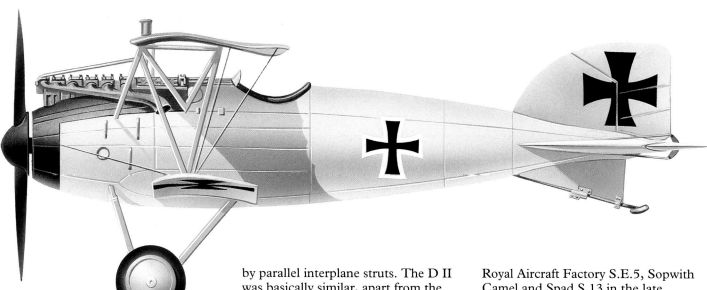

The first Albatros fighter was the excellent D I with virtually identical but staggered upper and lower wings connected toward their outboard ends by parallel interplane struts. The D II was basically similar, apart from the lowering of the upper wing to provide the pilot with improved forward and upward fields of vision. In an effort to improve manoeuvrability, designer Robert Thelen then moved to the D III with a revised and unstaggered wing cellule in which an increased-span upper wing was connected to the smaller and narrower-chord lower wing by V-section interplane struts.

The D III entered service in spring 1917 and proved most successful until the Allies introduced types such as the Royal Aircraft Factory S.E.5, Sopwith Camel and Spad S.13 in the late summer of the same year. During the course of the fighter's production, engine power was raised from 127- to 130-kW (170- to 175-hp) by increasing the compression ratio, and the radiator was shifted from the upper-wing centre section into the starboard upper wing so that the pilot would not be scalded if the radiator was punctured.

Albatros introduced the D V in May 1917 with features such as a still further lowered upper wing, a modified rudder, a revised aileron control system, and a larger spinner providing nose entry for a deeper elliptical rather than flat-sided plywood fuselage to reduce drag and so boost performance. Greater emphasis was then placed on this model and its D Va derivative with the upper wing and aileron control system of the D III. In fact the D V and D Va were outclassed by Allied fighters, and their lower wings were structurally deficient in the dive.

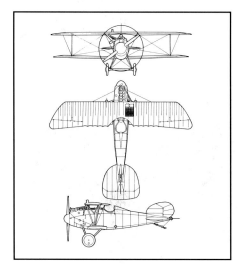

Albatros D Va

ALBATROS D III
Role: Fighter
Crew/Accommodation: One
Power Plant: One 175 hp Mercedes D.IIIa water-cooled inline
Dimensions: Span 9.05 m (29.76 ft); length 7.33 m (24 ft); wing area 20.5 m² (220.7 sq ft)
Weights: Empty 680 kg (1,499 lb); MTOW 886 kg (1,953 lb)
Performance: Maximum speed 175 km/h (109 mph) at 1,000 m (3,280 ft); operational ceiling 5,500 m (18,045 ft); endurance 2 hours
Load: Two 7.92 mm machine guns

Albatros D Va.

BRISTOL F.2 FIGHTER Series (United Kingdom)

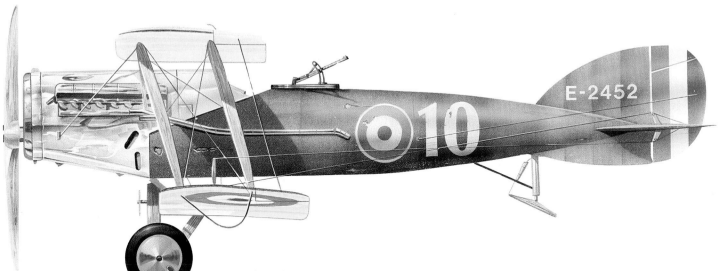

The F.2 Fighter was the best two-seat combat aircraft of World War I, even though it was designed in 1916 as a reconnaissance type. The design was an equal-span biplane of fabric-covered wooden construction, and in its original R.2A form it was planned round an 89-kW (120-hp) Beardmore engine. The availability of the 112-kW (150-hp) Hispano-Suiza engine resulted in the concept's revision as the slightly smaller R.2B sesquiplane, and further revision was then made so that the R.2B could also be fitted with the 142-kW (190-hp) Rolls-Royce Falcon engine. In August 1916, two prototypes and 50 production aircraft were ordered. Before the first prototypes flew in September 1916 the type had been reclassified as the F.2A fighter. All 50 aircraft were delivered together with the Falcon engine, and the F.2A entered service in February 1917.

The type's combat debut was disastrous, four out of six aircraft being lost to an equal number of Albatros D III fighters. But as soon as pilots learned to fly their F.2As as if they were single-seaters, with additional firepower provided by the gunner, the type became highly successful. The rest of the Fighter's 5,308-aircraft production run was of the F.2B variant with successively more powerful engines and modifications to improve fields of vision and combat-worthiness. Other designations were F.2C for a number of experimental re-enginings, F.2B Mk II for 435 new and reconditioned and tropicalized machines for army co-operation duties in the Middle East and India, Fighter Mk III for 80 strengthened aircraft delivered in 1926 and 1927, and Fighter Mk IV for Mk III conversions with strengthened structure and landing gear as well as a balanced rudder and automatic leading-edges slots. The RAF retired its last Fighters in 1932.

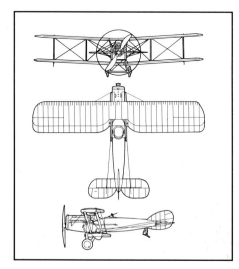

Bristol F.2B Fighter

BRISTOL F.2B
Role: Fighter
Crew/Accommodation: Two
Power Plant: One 275-hp Rolls-Royce Falcon III water-cooled inline
Dimensions: Span 11.96 m (39.25 ft); length 7.87 m (25.83 ft); wing area 37.6 m² (405 sq ft)
Weights: Empty 875 kg (1,930 lb); MTOW 1,270 kg (2,800 lb)
Performance: Maximum speed 201 km/h (125 mph) at sea level; operational ceiling 6,096 m (20,000 ft); endurance 3 hours
Load: Two or three .303 inch machine guns plus up to 54.4 kg (120 lb) of bombs

Bristol Fighter Mk III.

ROYAL AIRCRAFT FACTORY S.E.5 (United Kingdom)

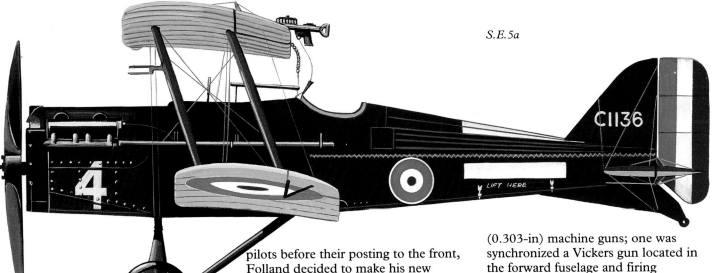

S.E.5a

The best aircraft to be designed by the Royal Aircraft Factory, and also the mount of several celebrated British aces of World War I, the S.E.5 was designed by H.P. Folland. Given the minimal levels of training received by pilots before their posting to the front, Folland decided to make his new aircraft easy to fly; thus a static inline engine was preferred to a rotary engine with all its torque problems, and a fair measure of inherent stability was built into the design. At the same time, Folland opted for an extremely strong airframe that was also easy to manufacture. Construction was entirely orthodox for the period, with fabric covering over a wooden primary structure. The result was a fighter that was an exceptionally good gun platform but, without sacrifice of structural strength, possessed good performance and adequate agility. The armament was an unusual variant on the standard pair of 7.7-mm (0.303-in) machine guns; one was synchronized a Vickers gun located in the forward fuselage and firing through the disc swept by the propeller, while the other was a Lewis located on a rail over the centre section and firing over the propeller. The Lewis gun could be pulled back and down along a quadrant rear extension of its rear so that the pilot could change ammunition drums. The S.E.5 was powered by a 112-kW (150-hp) Hispano-Suiza 8 inline and began to enter service in April 1917.

From the summer of the same year it was complemented and then supplanted by the S.E.5a version with a 149-kW (200-hp) engine. There were at first a number of teething problems with the engine and the Constantinesco synchronizer gear, but once these had been overcome the S.E.5a matured as a quite superlative fighter that could also double in the ground-attack role with light bombs carried under the wings. Total production was 5,205 aircraft.

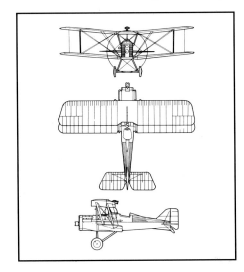

Royal Aircraft Factory S.E.5

ROYAL AIRCRAFT FACTORY S.E.5a
Role: Fighter
Crew/Accommodation: One
Power Plant: One 200 hp Wolseley W.4A Viper water-cooled inline
Dimensions: Span 8.12 m (26.63 ft); length 6.38 m (20.92 ft); wing area 22.84 m² (245.8 sq ft)
Weights: Empty 635 kg (1,399 lb); MTOW 880 kg (1,940 lb)
Performance: Maximum speed 222 km/h (138 mph) at sea level; operational ceiling 5,182 m (17,000 ft); endurance 2.5 hours
Load: Two .303 inch machine guns, plus up to 45 kg (100 lb) of bombs

The Royal Aircraft Factory S.E.5a was an outstanding fighter

SOPWITH CAMEL (United Kingdom)

Sopwith F.1 Camel

The Camel was clearly an evolution of the Pup's design concept and was in fact designed to supplant this type, but had all its major masses (engine, fuel/lubricant, guns/ammunition and pilot) located in the forward 2.1 m (7 ft) of the fuselage, on and around the centre of gravity to offer the least inertial resistance to agility. The type was therefore supremely manoeuvrable; the torque of the powerful rotary meant that a three-quarter turn to the right could be achieved as swiftly as a quarter turn to the left, but this also meant that the type could easily stall and enter a tight spin if it was not flown with adequate care.

In configuration Camel was a typical single-bay braced biplane with fixed tailwheel landing gear, and was built of wood with fabric covering except over the forward fuselage, which had light alloy skinning. The type was more formally known to its naval sponsors as the Sopwith Biplane F.1, the nickname deriving from the humped fuselage over the breeches of the two synchronized 7.7-mm (0.303-in) Vickers machine guns that comprised the armament. Production of 5,490 aircraft made this the most important British fighter of late 1917 and 1918. The type was powered in its production forms by a number of Bentley, Clerget, Gnome and Le Rhône rotary engines in the power class between 75 and 112 kW (100 and 150 hp), though some experimental variants had engines of up to 134-kW (180-hp) rating. Some F.1s were operated from ships, but a specialized derivative for this role was the 2F.1 with folding wings. Other variants were the F.1/1 with tapered wing panels, and the TF.1 trench fighter (ground-attack) model with a pair of 7.7-mm Lewis guns arranged to fire obliquely downward and forward through the cockpit floor, but neither of these entered production.

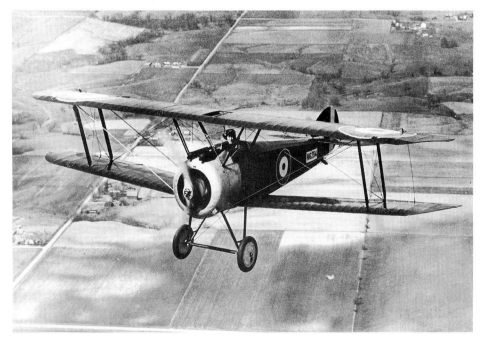

The Sopwith F.1 Camel.

SOPWITH F.1 CAMEL
Role: Fighter
Crew/Accommodation: One
Power Plant: One 130 hp Clerget 9B air-cooled rotary
Dimensions: Span 8.53 m (28 ft); length 5.71 m (18.75 ft); wing area 21.5 m² (231 sq ft)
Weights: Empty 436 kg (962 lb); MTOW 672 kg (1,482 lb)
Performance: Maximum speed 168 km/h (104.5 mph) at 3,048 (10,000 ft); operational ceiling 5,486 m (18,000 ft); endurance 2.5 hours
Load: Two .303 inch machine guns

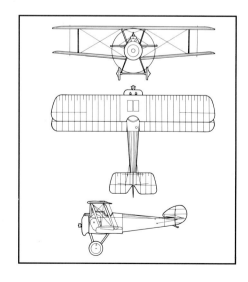

Sopwith F.1 Camel

17

FOKKER Dr I (Germany)

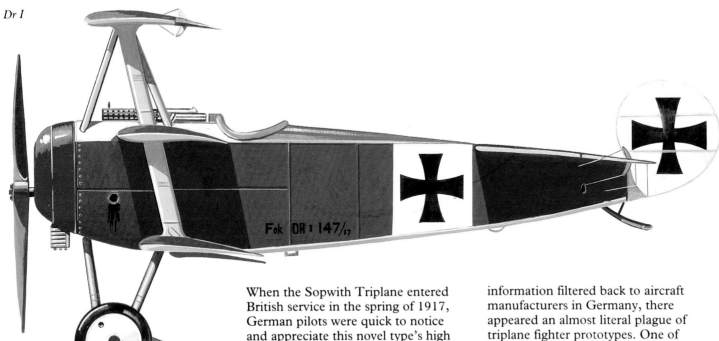

Dr I

When the Sopwith Triplane entered British service in the spring of 1917, German pilots were quick to notice and appreciate this novel type's high climb rate and excellent manoeuvrability. When this information filtered back to aircraft manufacturers in Germany, there appeared an almost literal plague of triplane fighter prototypes. One of these manufacturers was Fokker, whose V 3 prototype was designed by Reinhold Platz, who had become Fokker's chief designer after the death of Martin Kreutzer in a flying accident during June 1916.

Platz decided on a rotary-engined fighter of light weight for maximum agility rather than high performance, and to the typical Fokker fuselage and tail unit (welded steel tube structures covered in fabric) added triplane wings. These were of thick section and wooden construction, with plywood covering as far aft as the spar, and were cantilever units that did not require bracing wires or interplane struts. In flight the wings vibrated, however, and Platz added plank-type interplane struts on the V 4 second prototype that also incorporated a number of aerodynamic refinements. The type was put into production during the summer of 1917 as the F I, though this designation was soon altered to Dr I. The new triplane soon built up a phenomenal reputation, though this was the result not of the type's real capabilities, which were modest in the extreme, but of the fact that it was flown by a number of aces who had the skills to exploit the Dr I's superb agility in the defensive air combat waged by Germany over the Western Front. The type was grounded late in 1917 because of structural failures in the wing cellule, but with this defect remedied, the type was swiftly restored to service. Production ended in May 1918 after the delivery of about 300 aircraft.

Fokker Dr I

FOKKER Dr I
Role: Fighter
Crew/Accommodation: One
Power Plant: One 110 hp Oberursel U.R. II air-cooled rotary
Dimensions: Span 7.17 m (23.52 ft); length 5.77 m (18.93 ft); wing area 16 m² (172.2 sq ft)
Weights: Empty 405 kg (893 lb); MTOW 585 kg (1,289 lb)
Performance: Maximum speed 185 km/h (115 mph) at sea level; operational ceiling 5,975 m (19,603 ft); range 210 km (130 miles)
Load: Two 7.92 mm machine guns

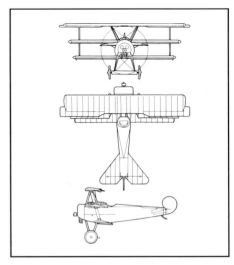

Fokker Dr I

FOKKER D VII (Germany)

Fokker D VII

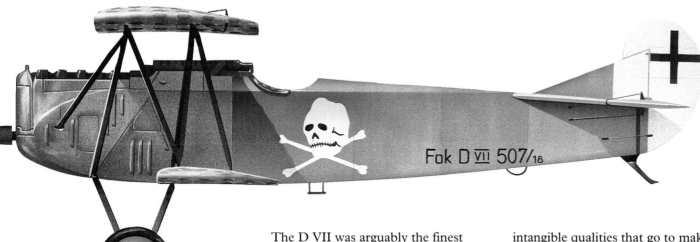

The D VII was arguably the finest fighter of World War I, for it was a package that featured great structrual strength, considerable agility, good firepower and a combination of those intangible qualities that go to making a 'pilot's aircraft'. The type was developed for Germany's first single-seat fighter competition, and the VII prototype made its initial flight just before this during January 1918. This machine had many similarities to the Dr I triplane in its fuselage, tail unit and landing gear. Reinhold Platz, designer of the D VII, intended his new fighter to offer considerably higher performance than that of the Dr I, and for this reason a more powerful inline engine, the 119-kW (160-hp) Mercedes D.III, was installed. This dictated the use of larger biplane wings. Despite the N-type interplane struts, these were cantilever units of Platz's favourite thick aerofoil section and wooden construction with plywood-covered leading edges.

As a result of its success in the competition, the type was ordered into immediate production as the D VII. Within three months, the type was in operational service, and some 700 had been delivered by the time of the Armistice. The type proved a great success in the type of defensive air fighting forced on the Germans at this stage of World War I.

It was particularly impressive in the high-altitude role as it possessed a good ceiling and also the ability to 'hang on its propeller' and fire upward at higher aircraft. Later examples were powered by the 138-kW (185-hp) BMW III inline for still better performance at altitude, and a number of experimental variants were built. Fokker returned to his native Netherlands at the end of the war, in the process smuggling back components for a number of D VIIs as a prelude to resumed construction.

The Fokker D VII was perhaps the best fighter of World War I

FOKKER D VII
Role: Fighter
Crew/Accommodation: One
Power Plant: One 160 hp Mercedes D.III water-cooled inline
Dimensions: Span 8.9 m (29.2 ft); length 6.95 m (22.8 ft); wing area 20.25 m² (218 sq ft)
Weights: Empty 700 kg (1,543 lb); MTOW 878 kg (1,936 lb)
Performance: Maximum speed 188 km/h (117 mph) at 1,000 m (3,281 ft); operational ceiling 6,100 m (20,013 ft); range 215 km (134 miles)
Load: Two 7.9 mm machine guns

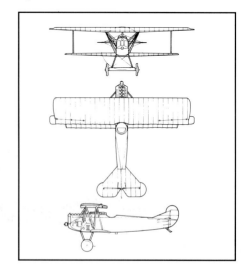

Fokker D VII

ARMSTRONG WHITWORTH SISKIN (United Kingdom)

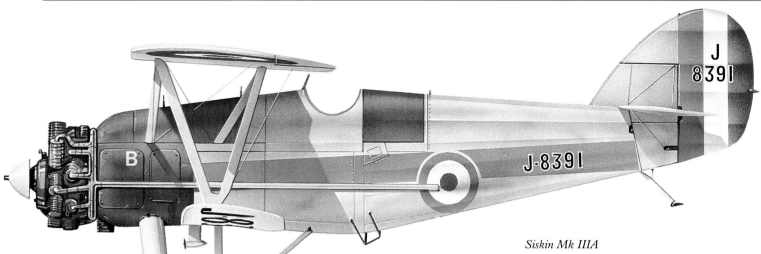

Siskin Mk IIIA

The Siskin was the mainstay of the Royal Air Force's fighter arm in the mid-1920s, and originated from the Siddeley Deasy S.R.2 of 1919. This was designed to use the 224-kW (300-hp) Royal Aircraft Factory 8 radial engine, a promising type whose final development was later passed to Siddeley Deasy but then put to one side so that the company could concentrate its efforts on the Puma.

The type first flew with the 239-kW (320-hp) A.B.C. Dragonfly radial and then as the Armstrong Siddeley Siskin with the definitive 242-kW (325-hp) Armstrong Siddeley Jaguar radial in 1921. The Siskin offered promising capabilities but, because the Air Ministry now demanded a primary structure of metal to avoid the possibility of wood shortages in the event of a protracted war, had to be recast as the Siskin Mk III of 1923 with a fabric-covered structure of aluminium alloy.

The 64 examples of the Siskin Mk III began to enter service in May 1924 with the 242-kW (325-hp) Jaguar III. These were later supplemented by 348 examples of the Siskin Mk IIIA, together with the supercharged Jaguar IV and 53 examples of the Siskin Mk IIIDC dual-control trainer variant. The Siskin Mk IIIB, Mk IV and Mk V were experimental and racing machines. In October 1924, Romania placed an order for the Siskin, however unfortunately the balance of the 65-aircraft contract was cancelled after the fatal crash of one of the first seven aircraft to be delivered. In British service, the Siskin was replaced by the Bristol Bulldog from October 1932, but in Canadian service the type was not replaced by the Hawker Hurricane until as late as 1939.

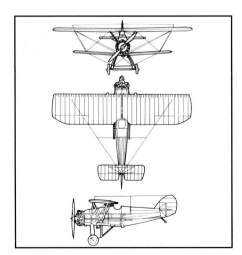

Armstrong Whitworth Siskin Mk IIIA

ARMSTRONG WHITWORTH SISKIN Mk IIIA
Role: Fighter
Crew/Accommodation: One
Power Plant: One 400 hp Armstrong Siddeley Jaguar IVS
Dimensions: Span 10.11 m (33.16 ft); length 7.72 m (25.33 ft); wing area 27.22 m² (293 sq ft)
Weights: Empty 997 kg (2,198 lb); MTOW, 1,260 kg (2,777 lb)
Performance: Maximum speed 227 km/h (141 mph) at sea level; operational ceiling 6,401 m (21,600 ft); endurance 2.75 hours
Load: Two .303 inch machine guns

Armstrong Whitworth Siskin is here represented by a Siskin Mk IIIAMk IIIA.

BOEING PW-9 and FB (U.S.A.)

Boeing PW-9D

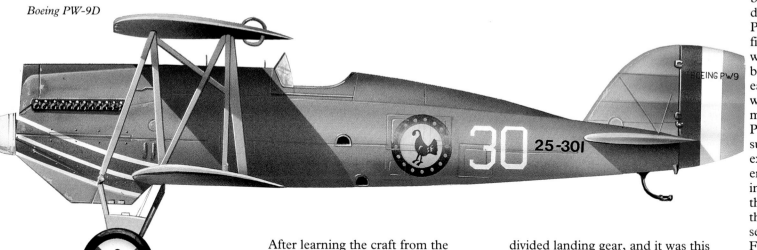

by 25 PW-9As with the D-12C and duplicated flying and landing wires, 40 PW-9Cs with the D-12D and revised fittings for the flying and landing wires, and 16 PW-9Ds with a balanced rudder that was retrofitted to earlier aircraft. A total of 14 FB-1s was ordered for the U.S. Marines, this model being virtually identical to the PW-9. Only 10 were delivered as such, the last four being used for experimental purposes with different engines (the Packard 1A-1500 inline in the first three and the Wright P-1 then Pratt & Whitney Wasp radial in the last) and designations in the sequence from FB-2 to FB-6 except FB-5. This was reserved for 27 aircraft with the Packard 2A-1500 engine, revised landing gear and in addition to this increased wing stagger.

After learning the craft from the manufacture of other company's designs, most notably the Thomas-Morse MB-3A, Boeing entered the fighter market with the Model 15 that first flew in June 1923 as an unequal-span biplane with a massive 324-kW (435-hp) Curtiss D-12 inline engine. The fixed landing gear was of the through-axle type, and while the flying surfaces were of wooden construction the fuselage was of welded steel tube; most of the airframe was covered in fabric. Performance was impressive, and after the type had been evaluated by the U.S. Army as the XPW-9, two more XPW-9s were ordered.

The second of these aircraft had divided landing gear, and it was this type that was ordered into production for the U.S. Army as the PW-9 series and the U.S. Marine Corps as the FB series. The 30 PW-9s were followed

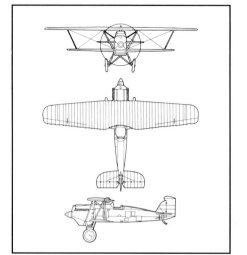

Boeing PW-9D

BOEING PW-9
Role: Fighter
Crew/Accommodation: One
Power Plant: One 435 hp Curtiss D-12 water-cooled inline
Dimensions: Span 9.75 m (32 ft); length 7.14 m (23.42 ft); wing area 24.15 m² (260 sq ft)
Weights: Empty 878 kg (1,936 lb); MTOW 1,415 kg (3,120 lb)
Performance: Maximum speed 256 km/h (159.1 mph) at sea level; operational ceiling 5,768 m (18,925 ft); range 628 km (390 miles)
Load: One .5 inch and one .303 inch machine guns

Boeing PW-9D.

CURTISS P-1 and F6C HAWK Series (U.S.A.)

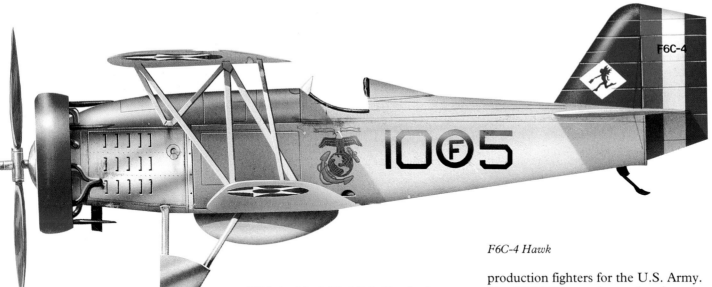

F6C-4 Hawk

With its Model L-18-1, Curtiss began the private-venture development of an advanced fighter that was to prove one of the decisive designs of the 1920s. The type first flew late in 1922, but was followed by only 25 PW-8 production fighters for the U.S. Army. The XPW-8B experimental variant with the 328-kW (440-hp) Curtiss D-12 engine introduced tapered wings and other alterations, resulting in an order for 10 examples of the P-1 production variant. This was then produced in a bewildering number of developed variants, of which the most significant were the 25 P-1As with detail improvements, the 25 P-1Bs with the 324-kW (435-hp) Curtiss V-1150-3 engine and larger-diameter wheels, and the 33 P-ICs with the V-1150-5 wheel brakes and provision for alternative ski landing gear. The type was also developed as the AT-4 advanced trainer. The type was based on the P-1A but engined with the 134-kW (180-hp) Wright-Hispano E, and of the 40 aircraft ordered, 35 became P-1Ds when re-engined with the V-1150, and the other five became AT-5s with the 164-kW (220-hp) Wright Whirlwind J-5 radial; they were later converted to P-1Es with the V-1150 engine. Some 31 AT-5As with a longer fuselage were ordered, but soon became P-1F fighters with the V-1150 engine.

The army's P-1 series was also attractive to the U.S. Navy, which ordered the type with the designation F6C. The F6C-1 was intended for land-based use by the U.S. Marine Corps and was all but identical with the P-1, but only five were delivered as such, while the four others were delivered as F6C-2s with carrier landing equipment including an arrester hook. The F6C-3 was a modified F6C-2, and these 35 aircraft were followed by 31 of the F6C-4 that introduced the 313-kW (420-hp) Pratt & Whitney R-1340 Wasp radial in place of the original D-12 inline.

Curtiss Hawk F6C-3.

CURTISS F6C-3
Role: Naval carrierborne fighter
Crew/Accommodation: One
Power Plant: One 400 hp Curtiss D.12 Conqueror water-cooled inline
Dimensions: Span 9.63 m (31.6 ft); length 6.96 m (22.83 ft); wing area 23.41 m² (252 sq ft)
Weights: Empty 980 kg (2,161 lb); MTOW 1,519 kg (3,349 lb)
Performance: Maximum speed 248 km/h (154 mph) at sea level; operational ceiling 6,187 m (20,300 ft); range 565 km (351 miles)
Load: Two .303 inch machine guns

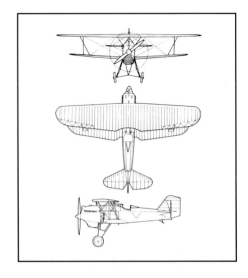

Curtiss F6C Hawk

BRISTOL BULLDOG (United Kingdom)

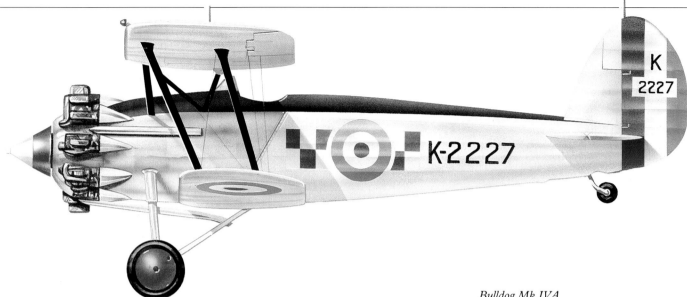

Bulldog Mk IVA

world altitude and time-to-height records. A second prototype introduced the lengthened fuselage of the Bulldog Mk II production model, which was powered by the 328-kW (440-hp) Bristol Jupiter VII radial, and had a number of modern features such as an oxygen system and short-wave radio.

The Bulldog Mk II entered service in June 1929, and the Bulldog became the U.K.'s most important fighter of the late 1920s and early 1930s. Total production was 312, including 92 basic Bulldog Mk IIs, 268 Bulldog Mk IIAs of the major production type with a strengthened structure and the 365-kW (490-hp) Jupiter VIIF engine, four Bulldog MK IIIs for Denmark with the Jupiter VIFH, two interim Bulldog MK IIIAs with the 418-kW (560-hp) Bristol Mercury IVS.2, 18 Bulldog Mk IVAs for Finland with strengthened ailerons and the 477-kW (640-hp) Mercury VIS.2, and 59 Bulldog TM trainers with a second cockpit in a rear fuselage section that could be replaced by that of the standard fighters in times of crisis.

By the mid-1920s, the performance of light day bombers such as the Fairey Fox was outstripping the defensive capabilities of fighters such as the Armstrong Whitworth Siskin, and in an effort to provide the British fighter arm with a considerably improved fighter, the Air Ministry in 1926 issued a fairly taxing specification for a high-performance day/night fighter armed with two fixed machine guns and powered by an air-cooled radial engine. Several companies tendered designs, and the Type 105 proposal from Bristol narrowly beat the Hawfinch from Hawker. The Type 105 was a conventional biplane of its period, with a fabric-covered metal structure, unequal-span wings and fixed landing gear of the spreader-bar type. The Bulldog Mk I prototype first flew in May 1927, and was later fitted with larger wings for attempts on the

Bristol Bulldog Mk IIA.

BRISTOL BULLDOG Mk IVA
Role: Fighter
Crew/Accommodation: One
Power Plant: One 640 hp Bristol Mercury VIS2 air-cooled radial
Dimensions: Span 10.26 m (33.66 ft); length 7.72 m (25.33 ft); wing area 27.31 m² (294 sq ft)
Weights: Empty 1,220 kg (2,690 lb); MTOW 1,820 kg (4,010 lb)
Performance: Maximum speed 360 km/h (224 mph) at sea level; operational ceiling 10,180 m (33,400 ft); endurance 2.25 hours
Load: Two .303 inch machine guns, plus up to 36 kg (80 lb) of bombs

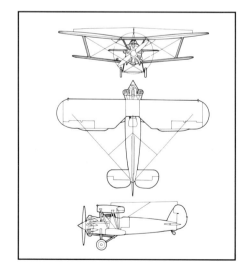

Bristol Bulldog Mk IIA

BOEING F4B and P-12 (U.S.A)

F4B-4

The U.S. Army ordered the type as the P-12, the first 10 aircraft being generally similar to the Model 89; later aircraft were 90 P-12Bs with revised ailerons and elevators, 95 P-12Cs similar to the F4B-2, 36 improved P-12Ds, 110 P-12Es with a semi-monocoque fuselage, and 25 P-12Fs with the Pratt & Whitney SR-1340 engine for improved altitude performance. There were also several experimental and even civil models, and also a number of export variants in a total production run of 586 aircraft. The aircraft began to enter American service in 1929, and were the mainstay of the U.S. Army's and U.S. Navy's fighter arms into the mid-1930s, and at that time they were replaced by more modern aircraft. Many aircraft were then used as trainers, mainly by the U.S. Navy, right up to the eve of the entry of the U.S.A. into World War II.

In an effort to produce replacements for the PW-9 and F2B/F3B series, Boeing developed its Models 83 and 89; the former had through-axle landing gear and an arrester hook, while the latter had divided main landing gear units and an attachment under the fuselage for a bomb. Both types were evaluated in 1928, and a hybrid variant with divided main units and an arrester hook was ordered for the U.S. Navy as the F4B-1 with tailskid landing gear. These 27 aircraft were followed by 46 F4B-2s with a drag-reducing cowling ring and through-axle landing gear with a tailwheel, 21 F4B-3s with a semi-monocoque fuselage and 92 F4B-4s with a larger fin and, to be found in the last 45 aircraft, a liferaft in the pilot's headrest.

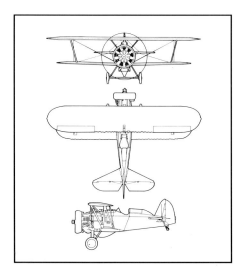

Boeing P-12E

BOEING F4B-4
Role: Naval carrierborne fighter bomber
Crew/Accommodation: One
Power Plant: One 500 hp Pratt & Whitney R-1340-D Wasp air-cooled radial
Dimensions: Span 9.14 m (30 ft); length 7.75 m (25.42 ft); wing area 21.18 m² (228 sq ft)
Weights: Empty 1,049 kg (2,312 lb); MTOW 1,596 kg (3,519 lb)
Performance: Maximum speed 301 km/h (187 mph) at sea level; operational ceiling 8,382 m (27,500 ft); range 941 km (585 miles)
Load: One .5 inch and one .303 inch machine guns, plus one 227 kg (500 lb) bomb

Boeing F4B-3.

24

CURTISS P-6 HAWK and F11C Series (U.S.A.)

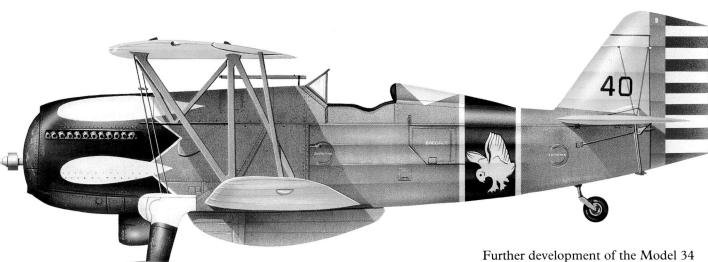

kW (700-hp) V-1570C Conqueror. This was the finest of the army's Hawk fighters, and was the Curtiss Model 35.

There were many experimental variants including the radial-engined P-3 and P-21, and the turbocharged P-5 and P-23.

The type also secured comparatively large export orders under the generic designation Hawk. The Hawk I was sold to the Netherlands East Indies (eight aircraft), Cuba (three) and Japan (one), while the same basic type with a Wright Cyclone radial was sold with the name Hawk II to Bolivia (nine), Chile (four plus licensed production), China (50), Colombia (26 float-equipped aircraft), Cuba (four), Germany (two), Norway (one), Siam (12) and Turkey (19).

In addition, the U.S. Navy ordered a version of the Hawk II with the 522-kW (700-hp) Wright R-1820-78 Cyclone radial and the designations F11C-2 (28 aircraft), and with manually operated landing gear that retracted into a bulged lower fuselage, another type, the BF2C-1 (27 aircraft).

Further development of the Model 34 (P-1 and F6C series) led to the P-6 series with the Curtiss V-1570 Conqueror engine. The development was pioneered in two P-1 conversions, namely the XP-6 with tapered wings and the XP-6A with the uptapered wings of the PW-8 and low-drag wing surfaced radiators. Both these aircraft were successful racers in 1927, and paved the way for the production series later on.

The main variants were the original P-6 of which nine were delivered with refined fuselage lines, the nine P-6As with Prestone-cooled engines, and the P-6E of which 46 were delivered in the winter of 1931-32 with the 522-

---

CURTISS P-6E
Role: Fighter
Crew/Accommodation: One
Power Plant: One 700 hp Curtiss V-1570C Conqueror water-cooled inline
Dimensions: Span 9.6 m (31.5 ft); length 6.88 m (22.58 ft); wing area 23.4 m² (252 sq ft)
Weights: Empty 1,231 kg (2,715 lb); MTOW 1,558 kg (3,436 lb)
Performance: Maximum speed 311 km/h (193 mph) at sea level; operational ceiling 7,285 m (23,900 ft); range 393 km (244 miles)
Load: Two .303 inch machine guns

Curtiss P-6E Hawk.

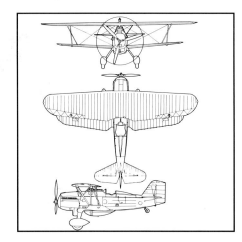

Curtiss P-6E

HAWKER FURY I and II biplanes (U.S.A.)

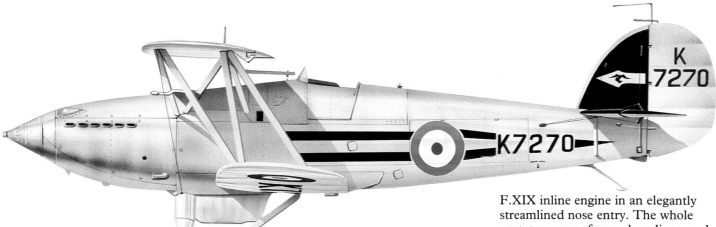

This single-seat fighter resulted from a 1927 requirement that led to the construction of prototype first flew with the 336-kW (450-hp) Bristol Jupiter radial specified by the Air

Ministry. The aircraft failed to win a production contract, but its experience with this prototype stood the company in good stead. After its Hart high-speed day bomber had entered service as a pioneer of a new breed of high-performance warplanes, Hawker developed as a private venture fighter prototype. Sydney Camm decided not to follow current Air Ministry preference for radial engines, but instead opted for the Rolls-Royce

F.XIX inline engine in an elegantly streamlined nose entry. The whole prototype was of very clean lines, and after purchase by the Air Ministry was renamed Fury.

Trials confirmed the type's capabilities as the first British fighter capable of exceeding 200 mph (322 km/h) in level flight, and the type was

placed in production for service from May 1931. The fighter was of metal construction covered with panels of light alloy and with fabric, and the powerplant was a single 391-kW (525-hp) Rolls-Royce Kestrel IIS engine driving a large two-blade propeller. Production of the Fury (later the Fury I) for the RAF totalled 118, though another 42 were built for export with a number of other engine types. Hawker developed the basic concept further in the Intermediate Fury and High-Speed Fury prototypes that led to the definitive Fury II with the 477-kW (640-hp) Kestrel VI and spatted wheels. This entered service in 1937, and the 98 aircraft were used as interim fighters pending large-scale deliveries of the Hawker Hurricane monoplane fighter. The Fury II was exported to Yugoslavia, which took 10 aircraft. The Nimrod was a naval equivalent; 100 were produced for British and Danish service.

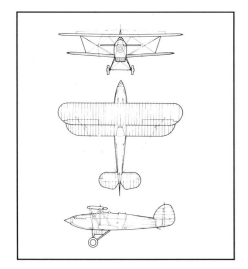

Hawker Fury Mk I

HAWKER FURY Mk II
Role: Interceptor
Crew/Accommodation: One
Power Plant: One 525 hp Rolls-Royce Kestrel IIS water-cooled inline
Dimensions: Span 9.15 m (30 ft); length 8.13 m (26.67 ft); wing area 23.4 m² (251.8 sq ft)
Weights: Empty 1,190 kg (2,623 lb); MTOW 1,583 kg (3,490 lb)
Performance: Maximum speed 309 km/h (192 mph) at 1,525 m (5,000 ft); operational ceiling 8,534 m (28,000 ft); range 491 km (305 miles)
Load: Two .303 inch machine guns

The Fury series was always notable for the elegance of its lines.

BOEING P-26 'PEASHOOTER' (U.S.A.)

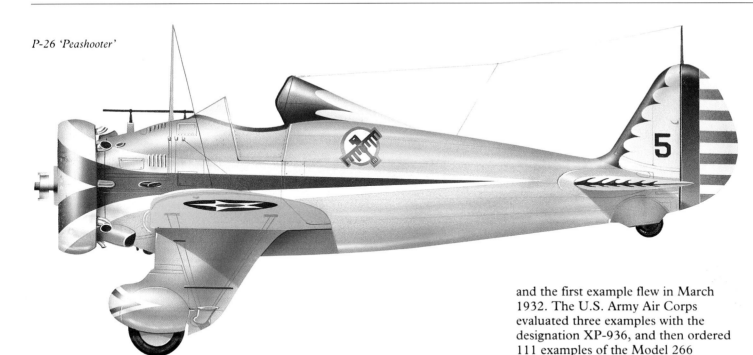

P-26 'Peashooter'

production version with a revised structure, flotation equipment, and radio. The P-26As were often known as 'Peashooters', and were delivered between January 1934 and June 1934.

Later aircraft had a taller headrest for improved pilot protection in the event of a roll-over landing accident, and were produced with the trailing-edge split flaps that had been developed to reduce landing speed; in-service aircraft were retrofitted with the flaps. Other variants were two P-26Bs with the fuel-injected R-1340-33 radial, and 23 P-26Cs with modified fuel systems.

Some 11 aircraft were also exported to China, and surplus American aircraft were later delivered to Guatemala and Panama. Ex-American aircraft operated by the Philippine Air Corps saw short but disastrous service in World War II.

and the first example flew in March 1932. The U.S. Army Air Corps evaluated three examples with the designation XP-936, and then ordered 111 examples of the Model 266

The Model 266 was a step, but only an interim step, towards the 'modern' monoplane fighter of all-metal construction that appeared in definitive form during the mid-1930s.

The Model 266 was indeed a monoplane fighter, but the wing was not a cantilever structure and had, therefore, to be braced by flying and landing wires. This bracing was in itself an obsolescent feature, and so too were the open cockpit and fixed landing gear, though the latter's main units were well faired. Boeing began work on its Model 248 private-venture prototype during September 1931,

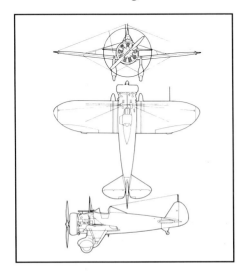

Boeing P-26A

BOEING P-26C
Role: Fighter
Crew/Accommodation: One
Power Plant: One 600 hp Pratt & Whitney R-1340-33 Wasp air-cooled radial
Dimensions: Span 8.52 m (27.96 ft); length 7.24 m (23.75 ft); wing area 13.89 m² (149 sq ft)
Weights: Empty 1,058 kg (2,333 lb); MTOW 1,395 kg (3,075 lb)
Performance: Maximum speed 378 km/h (235 mph) at sea level; operational ceiling 8,230 m (27,000 ft); range 1,022 km (635 miles)
Load: Two .5 inch machine guns, plus 90.8 kg (200 lb) of bombs

Boeing P-26A.

FIAT CR.32 and CR.42 FALCO (Italy)

CR.32

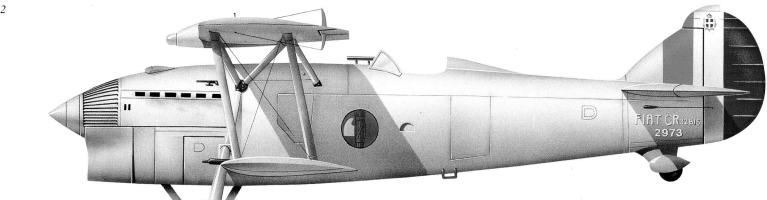

The CR.32 was Italy's finest fighter of the late 1930s, and marks one of the high points in biplane fighter design. The type was planned as successor to the CR.30 with smaller dimensions and reduced weight so that the type would have a comparably high level of agility but better overall performance on the same power. The prototype first flew in April 1933 with the 447-kW (600-hp) Fiat A.30 RAbis inline engine, and the successful evaluation of this machine led to production of slightly more than 1,300 aircraft in four series. These were about 350 CR.32 fighters with two 7.7-mm (0.303-in) machine guns, 283 CR.32bis close-support fighters with two 12.7-mm (0.5-in) and two 7.7-mm guns as well as provision for two 50-kg (110-lb) bombs, 150 CR.32ter fighters with two 12.7-mm (0.5-in) guns and improved equipment, and 337 CR.32quater fighters with radio and reduced weight. Another 100 or more of this last type were built in Spain as Hispano HA-132-L 'Chirri' fighters.

The Spanish Civil War led to the CR.42 Falco (Falcon) that first flew in prototype form during May 1938. This could be regarded as an aerodynamically refined version of the CR.32 with cantilever main landing gear units and more power in the form of a 626-kW (840-hp) Fiat A.74 R1C radial. More than 1,780 aircraft in five series were produced. The original CR.42 was armed with one 12.7-mm and one 7.7-mm machine guns. The CR.42AS was a close-support fighter with two 12.7-mm guns and two 10-kg (220-lb) bombs. The CR.42bis fighter was produced for Sweden with two 12.7-mm guns. The CR.42CN night fighter had two searchlights in underwing fairings. And the CR.42ter was a version of the CR.42bis with two 7.7-mm guns in underwing fairings.

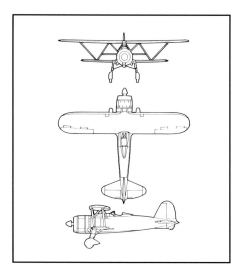

The Fiat CR.42bis Falco

FIAT CR.32bis
Role: Fighter
Crew/Accommodation: One
Power Plant: One 600 hp Fiat A30 RAbis water-cooled inline
Dimensions: Span 9.5 m (31.17 ft); length 7.47 m (24.51 ft); wing area 22.1 m² (237.9 sq ft)
Weights: Empty 1,455 kg (3,210 lb); MTOW 1,975 kg (4,350 lb)
Performance: Maximum speed 360 km/h (224 mph) at 3,000 m (9,840 ft); operational ceiling 7,700 m (25,256 ft); range 750 km (446 miles)
Load: Two 12.7 mm and two 7.7 mm machine guns, plus provision to carry up to 100 kg (220 lb) of bombs

The Fiat CR.42 bis Falco.

POLIKARPOV I-16 (U.S.S.R.)

I-16 Type 24

The I-16 was the first low-wing monoplane fighter to enter full service with retractable landing gear. The aircraft had a cantilever wing of metal construction married to a monocoque fuselage of wooden construction and, in addition to the manually retracted main landing gear unit, the type had long-span split ailerons that doubled as flaps. The type first flew in 1933 as the TsKB-12 with the 358-kW (480-hp) M-22 radial. The TsKB-12bis flew two months later with an imported 529-kW (710-hp) Wright SR-1820-F3 Cyclone radial and offered better performance. The handling qualities of both variants were tricky, because the short and very portly fuselage reduced longitudinal stability to virtually nothing, but its speed and rate of climb ensured that the machine was ordered into production, initially as an evaluation batch of 10 I-16 Type 1 fighters with the M-22.

Total production was 7,005 in variants with progressively more power and armament: the I-16 Type 4 used the imported Cyclone engine, the I-16 Type 5 had the 522-kW (700-hp) M-25 licensed version of the Cyclone and improved armour protection, the I-16 Type 6 was the first major production model and had the 544-kW (730-hp) M-25A, the I-16 Type 10 had the 559-kW (750-hp) M-25V and four rather than two 7.62-mm (0.3-in) machine-guns, the I-16 Type 17 was strengthened and had 20-mm cannon in place of the two wing machine guns plus provision for six 82-mm (3.2-in) rockets carried under the wings, the I-16 Type 18 had the 686-kW (920-hp) M-62 radial and four machine guns, the I-16 Type 24 had the 746-kW (1,000-hp) M-62 or 820-kW (1,100-hp) M-63 radial, strengthened wings and four machine guns, and the I-16 Types 28 and 30 that were reinstated in production during the dismal days of 1941 and 1942 had the M-63 radial. There were also SPB dive-bomber and I-16UTI dual-control trainer variants.

The I-16 was the world's first 'modern' monoplane fighter.

POLIKARPOV I-16 TYPE 24
Role: Fighter
Crew/Accommodation: One
Power Plant: One 1,000 hp Shvetsov M-62 air-cooled radial
Dimensions: Span 9 m (29.53 ft); length 6.13 m (20.11 ft); wing area 14.54 m² (156.5 sq ft)
Weights: Empty 1,475 kg (3,313 lb); MTOW 2,050 kg (4,519 lb)
Performance: Maximum speed 525 km/h (326 mph) at sea level; operational ceiling 9,000 m (29,528 ft); range 700 km (435 miles)
Load: Two 20 mm cannon and two 7.62 mm machine guns, plus six rocket projectiles

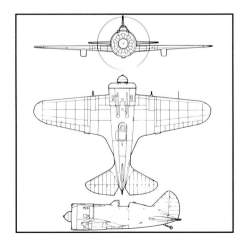

Polikarpov I-16 Type 24

DEWOITINE D.500 and D.510 Series (France)

D.510

The ungainly but impressive D.500 spanned the technological gap between the fabric-covered biplanes of the 1920s and the all-metal monoplane fighters of the mid-1930s. Designed as a successor to the Nieuport 62 and 622, the D.500 was of all-metal construction with a low-set cantilever wing, but these modern features were compromised by obsolescent items such as an open cockpit and fixed tailwheel landing gear the main legs of which carried large fairings. The D.500.01 prototype first flew in June 1932 with the 492-kW (660-hp) Hispano-Suiza 12Xbrs inline engine, and the type was ordered into production. The initial D.500 was produced to the extent of 101 aircraft, later aircraft with 7.5-mm (0.295-in) Darne machine guns in place of the original 7.7-mm (0.303-in) Vickers guns. There followed 157 D.501s with the 515-kW (690-hp) Hispano-Suiza 12Xcrs engine and a hub-mounted 20-mm cannon in addition to the two machine guns.

Projected variants were the D.502 catapult-launched floatplane fighter, the D.504 parachute trials aircraft, and the D.505 to D.509 with different engines. The main variant in service at the beginning of World War II was the D.510 based on the D.501 but powered by the 641-kW (860-hp) Hispano-Suiza 12Ycrs inline in a longer nose and featuring a number of refinements such as modified landing gear, greater fuel capacity and, in late aircraft, 7.5-mm MAC 1934 machine guns in place of the Darne weapons. Production of the D.510 totalled 120 aircraft in all.

An interesting experimental derivative was the D.511 of 1934: this had a smaller wing, cantilever main landing gear units, and the HS 12Ycrs engine. The type was never flown, as it was modified as the D.503 with the HS 12Xcrs and proving inferior to the D.501 aircraft.

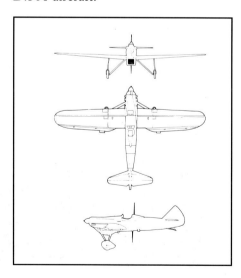

Dewoitine

DEWOITINE D.510

Role: Fighter

Crew/Accommodation: One

Power Plant: One 860 hp Hispano-Suiza 12Y crs .water-cooled inline

Dimensions: Span 12.09 m (39.67 ft); length 7.94 m (26.05 ft); wing area 16.5 m² (177.6 sq ft)

Weights: Empty 1,427 kg (3,145 lb); MTOW 1,915 kg (4,222 lb)

Performance: Maximum speed 402 km/h (250 mph) at 4,850 m (15,912 ft); operational ceiling 8,350 m (27,395 ft); range 985 km (612 miles)

Load: One 20 mm cannon and two 7.5 mm machine guns

Dewoitine D.500

MESSERSCHMITT Bf 109 (Germany)

Bf 109F-2

The Bf 109 was Germany's most important fighter of World War II in numerical terms, and bore the brunt of the air war until supplemented by the Focke-Wulf Fw 190 from 1941. The type went through a large number of production variants, and in common with other German aircraft was developed within these basic variants into a number of subvariants with factory- or field-installed modification packages.

The Bf 109 was designed from 1934 to provide the German Air Force with its first 'modern' fighter of all-metal stressed-skin construction with a low-set cantilever wing, retractable landing gear and enclosed cockpit. The first prototype flew in May 1935 with a 518-kW (695-hp) Rolls-Royce Kestrel inline, but the second had the 455-kW (610-hp) Junkers Jumo 210A for which the aircraft had been designed. The overall production figure has not survived, but it is thought that at least 30,500 aircraft were produced, excluding foreign production. The limited-number Bf 109A, B and C variants can be regarded mostly as pre-production and development models with differing Jumo 210s and armament fits. The Daimler-Benz DB 600A inline was introduced on the Bf 109D, paving the way for the first large-scale production variant, the Bf 109E produced in variants up to the E-9 with the 820-kW (1,100-hp) DB 601A. The Bf 109F introduced a more refined fuselage with reduced armament, and in addition was powered by the DB 601E or N in variants up to the F-6.

The most important production model was the Bf 109G with the DB 605 inline and provision for cockpit pressurization in variants up to the G-16. Later in the war there appeared comparatively small numbers of the Bf 109H high-altitude fighter with increased span in variants up to the H-1, and the Bf 109K improved version of the Bf 109G with the DB 605 inline in variants up to the K-14.

MESSERSCHMITT Bf 109G-6
Role: Fighter
Crew/Accommodation: One
Power Plant: One 1,475 hp Daimler-Benz DB605A water-cooled in line
Dimensions: Span 9.92 m (32.55 ft); length 9.02 m (29.59 ft); wing area 16.5 m² (172.75 sq ft)
Weights: Empty 2,700 kg (5,953 lb); MTOW 3,150 kg (6,945 lb)
Performance: Maximum speed 623 km/h (387 mph) at 7,000 m (22,967 ft); operational ceiling 11,750 m (38,551 ft); range 725 km (450 miles)
Load: One 30 mm cannon, two 20 mm cannon and two 13 mm machine guns, plus a 500 kg (1,102 lb) bomb

Bf 109F.

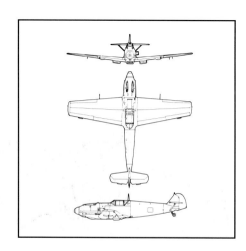

Messerschmitt Bf 109E-3

HAWKER HURRICANE (United Kingdom)

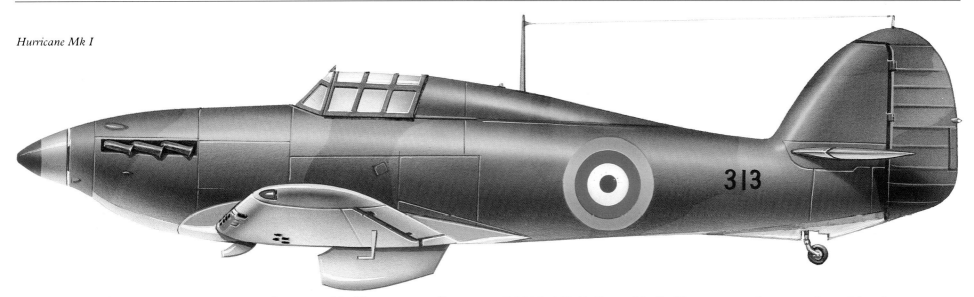

Hurricane Mk I

The Hurricane was the first British example of the 'modern' monoplane fighter, even though it lacked the stressed-skin construction of later machines such as the Supermarine Spitfire. The initial design was created as a private venture, and offered such advantages over current biplane fighters that a 1934 specification was written round it. The prototype first flew in November 1935 and revealed itself as a mix of advanced features (retractable landing gear, flaps and an enclosed cockpit) and an obsolescent structure of light alloy tube covered in fabric. This last did facilitate construction and repair, but limited the Hurricane's longer-term development potential despite an overall production total of 14,232 aircraft.

The Hurricane Mk I entered service in December 1937 with an armament of eight 7.7-mm (0.303-in) machine guns and the 768-kW (1,030-hp) Rolls-Royce Merlin II inline driving a two-blade propeller, and in the Battle of Britain was the RAF's most important and successful fighter with the 767-kW (1,029-hp) Merlin III driving a three-blade propeller. British production of 3,164 Mk Is was complemented by 140 Canadian-built Hurricane Mk Xs and a few Belgian- and Yugoslav-produced machines. Adoption of the 954-kW (1,280-hp) Merlin XX resulted in the Hurricane Mk II, of which 6,656 were produced in the U.K. in variants such as the Mk IIA with eight 7.7-mm machine-guns, the Mk IIB with 12 such guns and provision for underwing bombs, the Mk IIC based on the Mk IIB but with four 20-mm cannon, and the Mk IID with two 40-mm cannon in the anti-tank role; Canadian production amounted to 937 similar Hurricane Mks X, XI and XII aircraft. The final version was the Hurricane Mk IV, of which 2,575 were built with the 1208-kW (1,620-hp) Merlin 24 or 27 and a universal wing allowing the use of any of the standard armament combinations. About 825 aircraft were converted into Sea Hurricane Mks I and II.

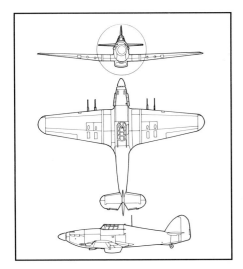

Hawker Hurricane Mk IIB

HAWKER HURRICANE Mk II B
Role: Fighter bomber
Crew/Accommodation: One
Power Plant: One 1,280 hp Rolls-Royce Merlin XX water-cooled inline
Dimensions: Span 12.19 m (40 ft); length 9.75 m (32 ft); wing area 23.9 m² (257.5 sq ft)
Weights: Empty 2,495 kg (5,500 lb); MTOW 3,311 kg (7,300 lb)
Performance: Maximum speed 722 km/h (342 mph) at 6,706 m (22,000 ft); operational ceiling 10,973 m (36,000 ft); range 772.5 km (480 miles) on internal fuel only
Load: Twelve .303 inch machine guns, plus up to 454 kg (1,000 lb) bombload

The Hawker Hurricane was the RAF's first 'modern' monoplane fighter.

NAKAJIMA Ki-27 'NATE' (Japan)

Ki-27 'Nate'

The Ki-27 was the Imperial Japanese Army Air Force's equivalent to the Navy's Mitsubishi A5M, and though it was an interim 'modern' fighter with

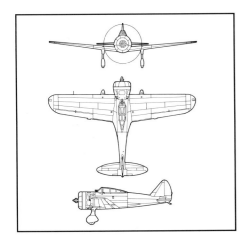

Nakajima Ki-27b 'Nate'

fixed landing gear (selected because of its light weight) it had more advanced features such as flaps and an enclosed cockpit. The type was evolved from the company's private-venture Type PE design, and the first of two prototypes flew in October 1936 with the 485-kW (650-hp) Nakajima Ha-1a radial. Flight trials with the prototypes confirmed the Ki-27's superiority to competing fighters, and 10 examples of the type with a modified clear-vision canopy were ordered for evaluation. These aircraft proved highly effective, and the first full-production type was ordered with the

company designation Ki-27a and the service designation Army Type 97 Fighter Model A.

The production programme lasted from 1937 to 1942 and totalled 3,384 aircraft in the original Ki-27a and modestly improved Ki-27b variants. The Ki-27a had an uprated Ha-1b (Army Type 97) engine and a metal-faired canopy, while the Ki-27b reverted to the clear-vision canopy and featured light ground-attack capability in the form of the four 25-kg (55-lb) bombs that could be

carried under the wings. A number of the fighters were converted as two-seat armed trainers, and two experimental lightweight fighters were produced with the designation Ki-27 KAI. The Ki-27 was used operationally up to 1942, when its light structure and poor armament forced its relegation to second-line duties. The type was initially known to the Allies in the China-Burma-India theatre as the 'Abdul', but 'Nate' later became the standard reporting name.

NALAJIMA Ki-27 'NATE'
Role: Fighter
Crew/Accommodation: One
Power Plant: One 710 hp Nakajima Ha-1b air-cooled radial
Dimensions: Span 11.3 m (37.07 ft); length 7.53 m (24.7 ft); wing area 18.6 m² (199.7 sq ft)
Weights: Empty 1,110 kg (2.447 lb); MTOW 1,650 kg (3,638 lb)
Performance: Maximum speed 460 km/h (286 mph) at 3,500 m (11,480 ft); operational ceiling 8,600 m (28,215 ft); range 1,710 km (1,050 miles)
Load: Two 7.7-mm machine guns, plus up to 100 kg (220 lb) of bombs

The Nakajima Ki-27.

CURTISS P-36 MOHAWK and HAWK 75 (U.S.A.)

P-36C

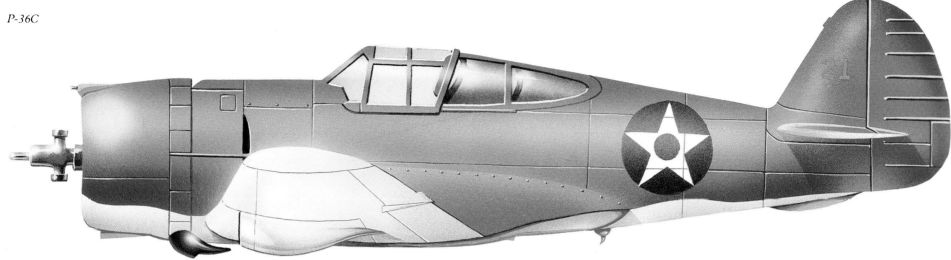

In 1934 Curtiss decided on the private-venture design of a modern fighter that might interest the U.S. Army Air Corps as a successor to the Boeing P-26 and would also have considerable export attractions.

The Model 75 prototype first flew in May 1935 as a low-wing monoplane of all-metal construction with an enclosed cockpit, retractable landing gear and a 671-kW (900-hp) Wright XR-1670-5 radial. The type was evaluated by the USAAC as the Model 75B with the 634-kW (750-hp) Wright R-1820 radial, but was initially beaten for a production order by the Seversky prototype that became the P-35.

The Curtiss machine was reworked into the Model 75E with the 783-kW (1,050-hp) Pratt & Whitney R-1830-13 derated to 708 kW (950 hp) and then re-evaluated as the Y1P-36. This was clearly a superior fighter, and in July 1937 the type was ordered into production as the P-36A with the fully rated version of the R-1830-13 driving a constant-speed propeller. Some 210 of the type were ordered, but only 31 were completed to P-36C standard with the 895-kW (1,200-hp) R-1830-17 engine and the two fuselage-mounted guns (one of 12.7-mm/0.5-in and the other of 7.62-mm/0.3-in calibre) complemented by two wing-mounted 7.62-mm guns.

The type was exported in fairly large numbers as the H75A, principally to France and the United Kingdom, but in smaller numbers to other countries. British aircraft were named Mohawk and comprised four main variants. Some 30 repossessed Norwegian aircraft were taken in charge by the Americans with the designation P-36G. In addition to this, Curtiss developed a less advanced version as the Hawk 75, in the main similar to the pre-production Y1P-36 but with a lower-powered 652-kW (875-hp) Wright GR-1820 radial and fixed landing gear.

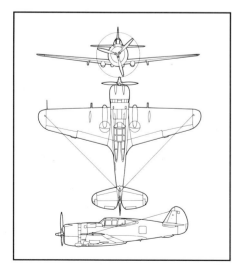

Curtiss P-36C

CURTISS P-36C (RAF MOHAWK)
Role: Fighter
Crew/Accommodation: One
Power Plant: One 1,200 hp Pratt & Whitney R-1830-17 Twin Wasp air-cooled radial
Dimensions: Span 11.35 m (37.33 ft); length 8.72 m (28.6 ft); wing area 21.92 m² (236 sq ft)
Weights: Empty 2,095 kg (4,619 lb); MTOW 2,790 kg (6,150 lb)
Performance: Maximum speed 501 km/h (311 mph) at 3,048 m (10,000 ft); operational ceiing 10,272 m (33,700 ft); range 1,320 km (820 miles) at 322 km/h (200 mph) cruise
Load: Four .303 inch machine guns

Curtiss P-36C.

SUPERMARINE SPITFIRE and SEAFIRE (United Kingdom)

Spitfire Mk IX

The Spitfire was the most important British fighter of World War II and remained in production right through the conflict for a total of 20,334 aircraft bolstered by 2,556 new-build Seafire naval fighters. The prototype first flew in March 1936 with a 738-kW (900-hp) Rolls-Royce Merlin C engine, and was soon ordered into production as the Spitfire Mk I with the 768-kW (1,030-hp) Merlin II and eight 7.7-mm (0.303-in) machine guns or, in the Mk IB variant, four machine guns and two 20-mm cannon; the suffix A indicated eight 7.7-mm machine-guns, B four such machine-guns and two 20-mm cannon, C four cannon, and E two cannon and two 12.7-mm (0.5-in) machine-guns.

Major fighter variants with the Merlin engine were the initial Mk I, the Mk II with the 876-kW (1,175-hp) Merlin XII, the Mks VA, VB and VC in F medium- and LF low-altitiude forms with the 1974-kW (1,440-hp) Merlin 45 or 1096-kW (1,470-hp) Merlin 50, the HF.Mk VI high-altitude interceptor with the 1055-kW (1,415-hp) Merlin 47 and a pressurized cockpit, the HF.Mk VII with the two-stage Merlin 61, 64 or 71, the LF, F and HF.Mk VIII with the two-stage Merlin 61, 63, 66 or 70 but an unpressurized cockpit, the LF, F and HF.Mk IX using the Mk V airframe with the two-stage Merlin 61, 63 or 70, the LF and F.Mk XVI using the Mk IX airframe with a cutdown rear fuselage, bubble canopy and Packard-built Merlin 226.

The Spitfire was also developed in its basic fighter form with the larger and more powerful Rolls-Royce Griffon inline, and the major variants of this sequence were the LF.Mk XI with the 1294-kW (1,735-hp) Griffon II or IV, the LF and F.Mk XIV with the 1529-kW (2,050-hp) Griffon 65 or 66 and often with a bubble canopy, the F.Mk XVIII with the two-stage Griffon and a bubble canopy, the F. Mk 21 with the Griffon 61 or 64, the F.Mk 22 with the 1771-kW (2,373-hp) Griffon 85 driving a contra-rotating propeller unit, and the improved F.Mk 24.

The Spitfire was also used as a unarmed reconnaissance type, the major Merlin-engined types being the Mks IV, X, XI and XIII, and the Griffon-engined type being the Mk XIX. The Seafire was the naval counterpart to the Spitfire, the main Merlin engined versions being the Mks IB, IIC and III, and the Griffon-engined versions being the Mks XV, XVII, 45, 46 and 47.

Supermarine Spitfire F.Mk XIV

SUPERMARINE SPITFIRE F.Mk XIV E
Role: Fighter
Crew/Accommodation: One
Power Plant: One 2,050 hp Rolls-Royce Griffon 65 water-cooled inline
Dimensions: Span 11.23 m (36.83 ft); length 9.96 m (32.66 ft); wing area 22.48 m² (242 sq ft)
Weights: Empty 2,994 kg (6,600 lb); MTOW 3,856 kg (8,500 lb)
Performance: Maximum speed 721 km/h (448 mph) at 7,925 m (26,000 ft); operational ceiling 13,106 m (43,000 ft); range 740 km (460 miles) on internal fuel only
Load: Two 20 mm cannon and two .303 machine guns, plus up to 454 kg (1,000 lb) of bombs

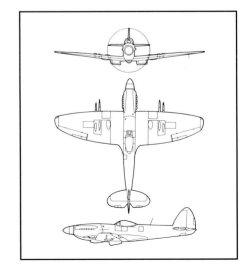

Supermarine Spitfire F.Mk 24

DEWOITINE D.520 (France)

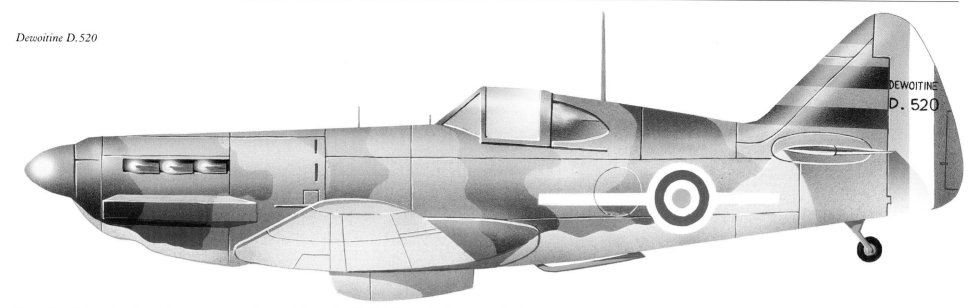

Dewoitine D.520

Dewoitine's first 'modern' low-wing monoplane fighter was the D.513 that first flew in January 1936 with a 641-kW (860-hp) Hispano-Suiza 12Ycrs inline. The type introduced advanced features such as an enclosed cockpit and retractable landing gear, but its low performance and severe instability problems proved very disappointing. The type was extensively revised but still had problems, so it was abandoned.

The company used the lessons learned from the D.513 fiasco in the creation of the D.520 which proved a far more satisfactory type and was ordered in substantial numbers. One of the most advanced fighters to serve with the French Air Force in the disastrous early campaign of 1940, the D.520 was a modern fighter of considerably trimmer and more pleasing lines than the D.513. It embodied an enclosed cockpit, trailing-edge flaps, retractable tailwheel landing gear and a variable-pitch propeller for the engine located in a much cleaner nose installation.

The D520.01 prototype first flew in October 1938 with the 664-kW (890-hp) Hispano-Suiza 12Y-21 inline, though the two following prototypes had wing, vertical tail and cockpit canopy modifications as well as the 746-kW (1,000-hp) HS 12Y-51 and 619-kW (830-hp) HS 12Y-31 engines respectively. Substantial orders were placed for the D.520 with the 686-kW (920-hp) HS 12Y-45 or -49, but only 403 aircraft had been delivered before the fall of France in June 1940. The in-service fighters did well in combat with German aircraft, and 478 aircraft were built for the Vichy French Air Force. Surviving aircraft remained up to the early 1950s. There were several experimental variants including the very promising D.524 with the 895-kW (1,200-hp) HS 12Y-89.

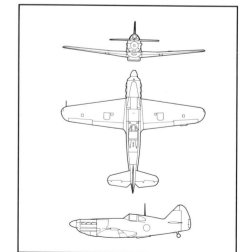

Dewoitine D.520.

DEWOITINE D.520
Role: Fighter
Crew/Accommodation: One
Power Plant: One 920 hp Hispano-Suiza 12Y45 water-cooled inline
Dimensions: Span 10.2 m (33 ft); length 8.76 m (28 ft); wing area 15.95 m² (171.7 sq ft)
Weights: Empty 2,092 kg (4,612 lb); MTOW 2,783 kg (6,134 lb)
Performance: Maximum speed 535 km/h (332 mph) at 6,000 m (19,685 ft); operational ceiling 11,000 m (36,090 ft); range 900 km (553 miles)
Load: One 20 mm cannon and four 7.5 mm machine guns

Dewoitine D.520

BLOCH M.B. 151 and M.B. 152 (France)

M.B. 152 C1

The M.B. 151 was one of France's first 'modern' monoplane fighters, and resulted from the unsuccessful M.B. 150 prototype produced to meet a 1934 requirement. The M.B.150 could not at first be persuaded to fly, but after it had been fitted with a larger wing, revised landing gear and a 701-kW (940-hp) Gnome-Rhône 14N radial, the type first flew in October 1937. In 1938 further improvement in flight performance was achieved with a slightly larger wing and the Gnome-Rhône 14N-7 engine, and a pre-production batch of 25 M.B. 151 fighters was ordered with slightly reduced wing span and the 695-kW (920-hp) Gnome-Rhône 14N-11 radial. The first of these flew in August 1938, and there followed 115 production aircraft with the identically rated Gnome-Rhône 14N-35 radial.

The type was deemed to lack the performance required of a first-line fighter, and was generally used as a fighter trainer. An improved version was developed as the M.B. 152 with the more powerful 768-kW (1,030-hp) Gnome-Rhône 14N-25 or 790-kW (1,060-hp) Gnome-Rhône 14N-49. Production was slow, and only a few M.B. 152s were combat–ready in time for the German invasion of May 1940; more than 30 aircraft had been delivered by January 1940, but most lacked the right propeller. The airworthy examples served with success during the German invasion of mid-1940, and then remained operational with the Vichy French air force. Some aircraft were used by the Luftwaffe as trainers, and 20 were passed to Romania.

The Bloch M.B. 151.

BLOCH M.B. 152
Role: Fighter
Crew/Accommodation: One
Power Plant: One 1,000 hp Gnome-Rhône 14N-25 air-cooled radial
Dimensions: Span 10.54 m (34.58 ft); length 9.1 m (29.86 ft); wing area 17.32 m² (186.4 sq ft)
Weights: Empty 2,158 kg (4,758 lb); MTOW 2,800 kg (6,173 lb)
Performance: Maximum speed 509 km/h (316 mph) at 4,500 m (14,765 ft); operational ceiling 10,000 m (32,808 ft); range 540 km (335 miles)
Load: Two 20 mm cannon and two 7.5 mm machine guns

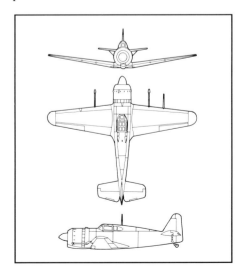

Bloch M.B. 155

BOULTON PAUL DEFIANT (United Kingdom)

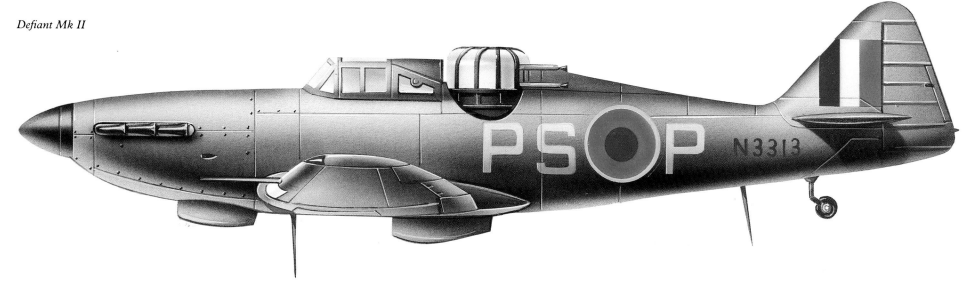

Defiant Mk II

In the mid-1930s there was considerable enthusiasm among Royal Air Force planners for the two-seat fighter in which all the armament would be concentrated in a power-operated turret. Such a fighter, its protagonists claimed, would be able to penetrate into enemy bomber streams and wreak havoc. A first expression of this concept was found in the Hawker

Demon, of which 59 were manufactured in 1934 by Boulton Paul with a Frazer-Nash turret. The company was therefore well placed to respond to a 1935 requirement for a more advanced two-seat turret fighter. The P.82 design was for a trim fighter of the 'modern' monoplane type, little larger than current single-seaters and fitted with a four-gun turret immediately aft of the cockpit. The first of two Defiant prototypes flew in

August 1937 with a 768-kW (1,030-hp) Rolls-Royce Merlin I inline engine, and the Defiant Mk I fighter began to enter service in December 1939.

After early encounters with German warplanes, in which the Defiant scored some success because of the novelty of its layout, operations soon revealed the inadequacy of a type in which the turret's weight and drag imposed severe performance and handling limitations and also left the pilot without fixed forward-firing

armament. It was decided to convert existing fighters to Defiant NF.Mk IA night fighter standard with primative AI.Mk IV or VI radar. Mk I production totalled 723, and another 210 night fighters were built as Defiant NF.Mk IIs with the more powerful Merlin XX engine and larger vertical tail surfaces. Many were later converted to Defiant TT.Mk I target-tugs and another 140 were built as such; similarly converted Mk Is became Defiant TT.Mk IIIs. Total production was 1,075.

Boulton Paul Defiant Mk I

BOULTON PAUL DEFIANT Mk II
Role: Night fighter
Crew/Accommodation: Two
Power Plant: One 1,280 hp Rolls-Royce Merlin XX water-cooled inline
Dimensions: Span 11.99 m (39.33 ft); length 10.77 m (35.33 ft); wing area 23.23 m² (250 sq ft)
Weights: Empty 2,850 kg (6,282 lb); MTOW 3,773 kg (8,318 lb)
Performance: Maximum speed 507 km/h (315 mph) at 5,029 m (16,500 ft); operational ceiling 9,251 m (30,350 ft); range 748 km (465 miles)
Load: Four .303 inch machine guns in power-operated turret.
Note: The Defiant Mk III was retrofitted to embody AIMk4 radar.

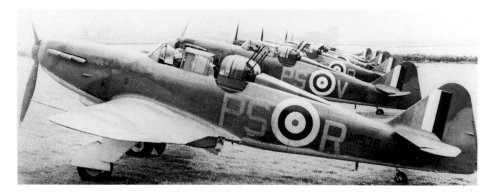

Boulton Paul Defiant Mk I

GRUMMAN F4F WILDCAT (U.S.A.)

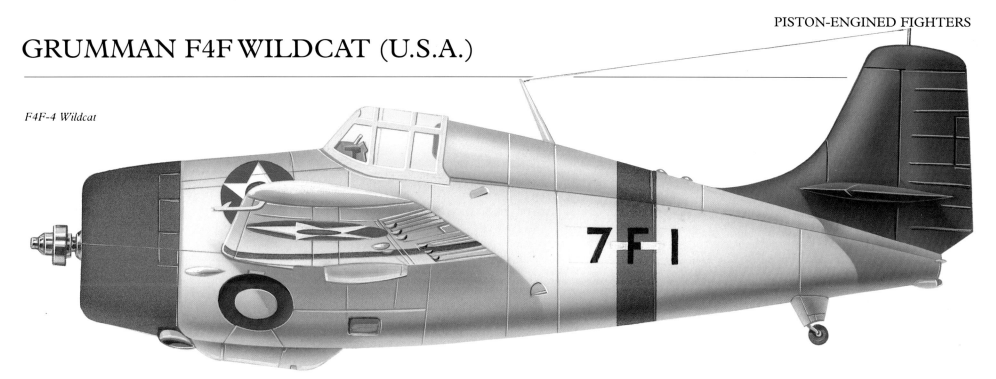

F4F-4 Wildcat

The F4F designation was first used for the G-16 biplane ordered as the XF4F-1 in competition to the Brewster monoplane prototype that was accepted for service as the F2A Buffalo carrierborne fighter. Grumman did not build the biplane prototype, but instead reworked the design as the G-18 monoplane. Re-evaluation of Grumman's proposal led the U.S. Navy to call for an XF4F-2 monoplane prototype, and this first flew in September 1937 with a 783-kW (1,050-hp) Pratt & Whitney R-

1830-66 Twin Wasp radial. This initial model was judged slightly inferior to the Buffalo, but was revised as the G-36 with a redesigned tail, a larger wing and the XR-1830-76 engine.

This XF4F-3 first flew in March 1939, and its performance and handling were so improved that the type was ordered as the F4F-3, the British taking a similar version as the Martlet Mk I; the armament was four 12.7-mm (0.5 in) machine guns and production totalled 369 excluding 95

F4F-3As with the R-1830-90 engine. The F4F/Martlet was the first Allied carrierborne fighter able to meet land-based opponents on anything like equal terms, and proved invaluable during the early war years up to 1943 in variants such as the 1,169 examples of the F4F-4 (Martlet Mks II, III and IV) with wing folding, armour, self-sealing tanks and six rather than four machine guns, and the 21 examples of the F4F-7 unarmed long-range reconnaissance version. The Eastern Aircraft Division of General Motors built 1,060 of the FM-1 (Martlet Mk V) equivalent to the F4F-4 with the R-

1830-86 engine, four wing guns, and provision for underwing stores, and 4,127 of the FM-2 (Martlet Mk V) based on Grumman's XF4F-8 prototype with the 1007-kW (1,350-hp) Wright R-1820-56 Cyclone, taller vertical tail surfaces and, on the last 826 aircraft, provision for six 127-mm (5-in) rockets under the wings.

Grumman F4F-4 Wildcat.

GRUMMAN F4F-4 WILDCAT
Role: Naval carrierborne fighter
Crew/Accommodation: One
Power Plant: One 1,200 hp Pratt & Whitney R-1830-86 Twin Wasp air-cooled radial
Dimensions: Span 11.58 m (38 ft); length 8.76 m (28.75 ft); wing area 24.16 m² (260 sq ft)
Weights: Empty 2,624 kg (5,785 lb); MTOW 3,607 kg (7,952 lb)
Performance: Maximum speed 512 km/h (318 mph) at 5,913 m (19,400 ft); operational ceiling 10,638 m (34,900 ft); range 1,239 km (770 miles) on internal fuel only
Load: Six .5 inch machine guns

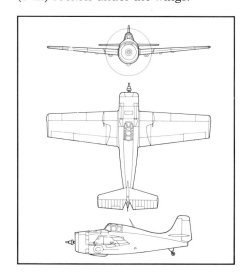

Grumman F4F-4 Wildcat

BRISTOL BEAUFIGHTER (United Kingdom)

Beaufighter Mk I

The Beaufighter was born of the Royal Air Force's shortage of heavy fighters (especially heavily armed night fighters and long-range escort fighters) as perceived at the time of the 'Munich crisis' late in 1938. The Type 156 was planned round the wings, tail unit and landing gear of the Type 152 Beaufort torpedo bomber married to a new fuselage and two Hercules radials.

The first of four prototypes flew in July 1939, and production was authorized with 1119-kW (1,500-hp) Hercules XI engines. Development of the Beaufighter at this time divided into two role-orientated streams. First of these was the night fighter as exemplified by the 553 Beaufighter Mk IFs with Hercules XIs, nose radar and an armament of four 20-mm nose cannon and six 7.7-mm (0.303-in) wing machine-guns. This model entered service in July 1940, and

further evolution led to the 597 Beaufighter Mk IIFs with 954-kW (1,280-hp) Rolls-Royce Merlin XX inlines, and finally the 879 Beaufighter Mk VIFs with 1245-kW (1,675-hp) Hercules VIs or XVIs and improved radar in a 'thimble' nose.

With its high performance and capacious fuselage, which made the installation of radar a comparatively simple matter, the Beaufighter night fighter provided the RAF with its first truly effective method of combating nocturnal German bombers. More significant in the longer term,

however, was the anti-ship version first developed as the 397 Beaufighter Mk ICs and then evolved via the 693 torpedo-carrying Beaufighter Mk VICs and 60 Beaufighter Mk VI (ITF)s with eight 27-kg (60-lb) rockets in place of the wing guns, to the 2,205 Beaufighter TF.Mk Xs with search radar and an armament of one torpedo plus light bombs or eight rockets. The 163 Beaufighter TF.Mk XIs were similar, while the 364 Beaufighter TF.Mk 21s were the Australian-built equivalents of the TF.Mk X.

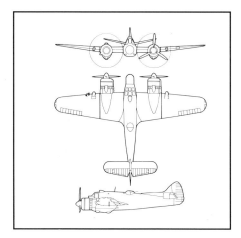

Bristol Beaufighter TF.Mk X

BRISTOL BEAUFIGHTER Mk IF
Role: Night fighter
Crew/Accommodation: Two
Power Plant: Two 1,400 hp Bristol Hercules XI air-cooled radials
Dimensions: Span 17.63 m (57.83 ft); length 12.60 m (41.33 ft); wing area 46.7 m² (503 sq ft)
Weights: Empty 6,382 kg (14,069 lb); MTOW 9,525 kg (21,000 lb)
Performance: Maximum speed 520 km/h (323 mph) at 4,572 m (15,000 ft); operational ceiling 8,839 m (29,000 ft); range 2,413 km (1,500 miles) internal fuel only
Load: Four 20 mm cannon and six .303 machine guns (interception guided by AI Mk IV radar)

TF.Mk X.

MACCHI MC.200 to MC.205 Series (Italy)

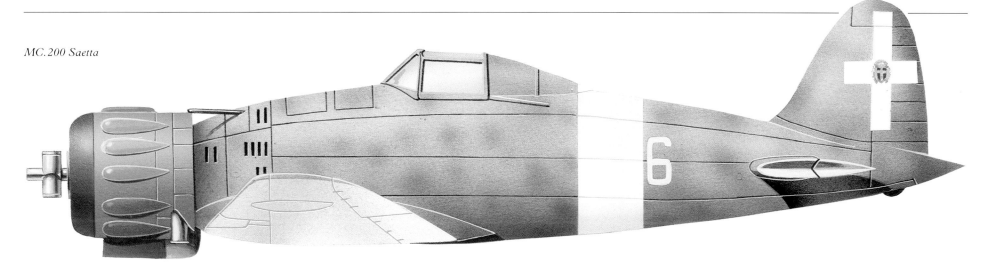

MC.200 Saetta

In 1936 the Italian Air Force belatedly realized that the day of the biplane fighter was effectively over, and requested the development of a 'modern' monoplane fighter with stressed-skin metal construction, a low-set cantilever monoplane wing, an enclosed cockpit and retractable landing gear. Macchi's response was the MC.200 Saetta (lightning) that first flew in December 1937 with the

649-kW (870-hp) Fiat A.74 RC 38 radial engine. The type was declared superior to its competitors during 1938 and ordered into production to a total of 1,153 aircraft in variants that 'progressed' from an enclosed to an open and eventually a semi-enclosed cockpit.

The MC.200 was a beautiful aircraft to fly, but clearly lacked the performance to deal with the higher-performance British fighters. There was no Italian inline engine that could offer the required performance, so the MC.202 Folgore (Thunderbolt) that flew in August 1940 with an enclosed

cockpit used an imported Daimler-Benz DB 601A engine. About 1,500 production aircraft followed, initially with imported engines but later with licence-built Alfa-Romeo RA.100 RC 41-I Monsone engines rated at 876-kW (1,175-hp). The MC.205V Veltro (Greyhound) was a development of the MC.202 with the 1100-kW (1,475-hp) DB 605A engine and considerably heavier armament. The

MC.205 was first flown in April 1942 but production had then to await availability of the licensed DB 605A, the RA.1050 RC 58 Tifone, so deliveries started only in mid-1943. Production amounted to 252, and most of these aircraft served with the fascist republic established in northern Italy after the effective division of Italy by the September 1943 armistice with the Allies.

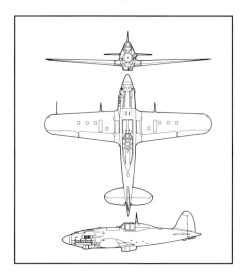

Macchi Mc.205V Veltro

MACCHI MC.205V VELTRO Series II
Role: Fighter
Crew/Accommodation: One
Power Plant: One 1,475 hp Fiat-built Daimler-Benz DB605A water-cooled inline
Dimensions: Span 10.58 m (34.71 ft); length 8.85 m (29.04 ft); wing area 16.8 m² (180.8 sq ft)
Weights: Empty 2,581 kg (5,690 lb); MTOW 3,224 kg (7,108 lb)
Performance: Maximum speed 642 km/h (399 mph) at 7.200 m (2,620 ft); operational ceiling 11,000 m (36,090 ft); range 950 km (590 miles)
Load: Two 200 mm cannon, plus up to 320 kg (706 lb) of bombs

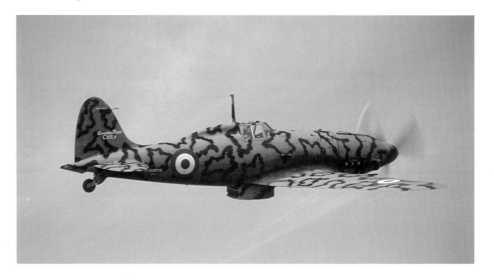

The Macchi MC.205V Veltro

CURTISS P-40 WARHAWK Family (U.S.A.)

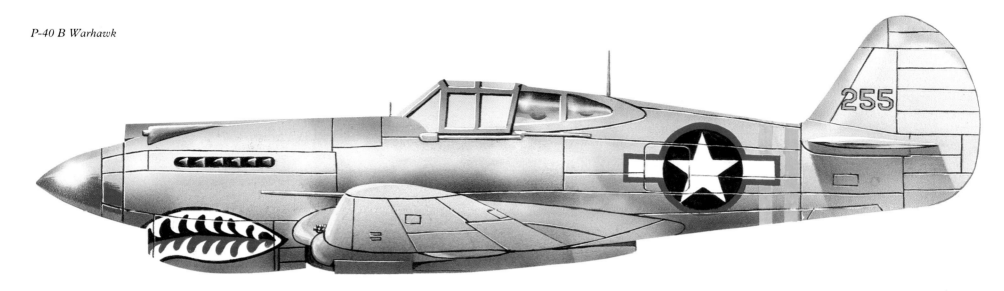

P-40 B Warhawk

The P-40 series was in no way an exceptional warplane, but nonetheless proved itself a more than adequate fighter-bomber. It was exceeded in numbers by only two other American fighters, the Republic P-47 Thunderbolt and North American P-51 Mustang. The basis for the P-40 series was the Model 75I, a Model 75/

XP-37A airframe modified to take the 858-kW (1,150-hp) Allison V-1710-11 inline engine. This became the first U.S. fighter to exceed 300 mph (483 km/h) in level flight, and the type was ordered by the U.S. Army Air Corps in modified form with the designation P-40 and the less powerful V-1710-33; export versions were the Hawk 81-A1 for France and Tomahawk Mk I for the UK.

Improved models were the P-40B (Tomahawk Mk IIA) with self-sealing

tanks, armour and better armament, the P-40C (Tomahawk Mk IIB) with improved self-sealing tanks and two more wing guns, the P-40D (Kittyhawk Mk I) with the 858-kW (1,150-hp) V-1710-39 with better supercharging to maintain performance to a higher altitude, and the P-40E with four wing guns plus the similar Kittyhawk Mk IA with six wing guns. The P-40 series had all along been limited by the indifferent supercharging of the V-1710, and this situation was remedied in the P-40F and generally similar P-40L

(Kittyhawk Mk II) by the adoption of the 969-kW (1,300-hp) Packard V-1650-1 (licence-built Rolls-Royce Merlin). The type's forte was still the fighter-bomber role at low altitude, and further developments included the P-40K (Kittyhawk Mk III) version of the P-40E with the V-1710-33 engine, the P-40M with the V-1710-71 engine, and the definitive P-40N (Kittyhawk Mk IV) with the V-1710-81/99/115 engine and measures to reduce weight significantly as a means of improving performance.

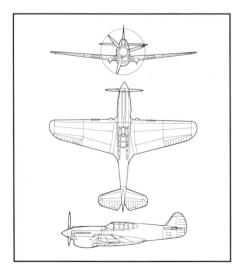

Curtiss P-40E Warhawk

CURTISS P-40F WARHAWK
Role: Fighter
Crew/Accommodation: One
Power Plant: One 1,300 hp Packard-built Rolls-Royce V-1650-1 Merlin water-colled inline
Dimensions: Span 11.38 m (37.33 ft); length 10.16 m (33.33 ft); wing area 21.93 m² (236 sq ft)
Weights: Empty 2,989 kg (6,590 lb); MTOW 4,241 kg (9,350 lb)
Performance: Maximum speed 586 km/h (364 mph) at 6,096 m (20,000 ft); operational ceiling 10,485 m (34,400 ft); range 603 km (375 miles)
Load: Six .5 inch machine guns, plus up to 227 kg (500 lb) of bombs

Curtiss P-40 Warhawk

FOCKE-WULF Fw 190 and Ta 152 (Germany)

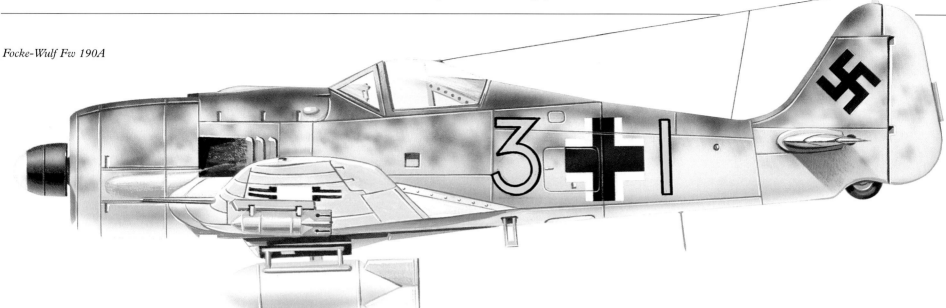

Focke-Wulf Fw 190A

The Fw 190 was Germany's best fighter of World War II, and resulted from the belief of designer Kurt Tank that careful streamlining could produce a radial-engined fighter with performance equal to that of an inline-engined type without the extra complexity and weight of the latter's water-cooling system. The first of three prototypes flew in June 1939, and an extensive test programme was required to develop the air cooling system and evaluate short- and long-span wings, the latter's additional 1.0 m (3 ft 3.7 in) of span and greater area reducing performance but boosting both agility and climb rate. This wing was selected for the Fw 190A

production type in a programme that saw the building of about 19,500 Fw 190s. The Fw 190A was powered by the BMW 801 radial, and was developed in variants up to the Fw 190A-8 with a host of subvariants optimized for the clear- or all-weather interception, ground-attack, torpedo attack and tactical reconnaissance roles, together with an immensely diverse armament.

The Fw 190B series was used to develop high-altitude capability with longer-span wings and a pressurized cockpit, and then pioneered the 1304-kW (1,750-hp) Daimler-Benz DB 603 inline engine. The Fw 190C was another high-altitude development

model with the DB 603 engine and a turbocharger. The next operational model was the Fw 190D, which was developed in role-optimized variants between Fw 190D-9 and Fw 190D-13 with the 1324-kW (1,776-hp) Junkers Jumo 213 inline and an annular radiator in a lengthened fuselage. The Fw 190E was a proposed reconnaissance fighter, and the Fw 190F series, which preceded the Fw 190D model, was a specialized ground-attack type based

on the radial-engined Fw 190A-4. Finally in the main sequence came the FW 190G series of radial-engined fighter-bombers evolved from the Fw 190A-5. An ultra-high-altitude derivative with longer-span wings was developed as the Jumo 213-engined Ta 152, but the only operational variant was the Ta 152H.

Focke-Wulf Fw 190

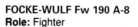

FOCKE-WULF Fw 190 A-8
Role: Fighter
Crew/Accommodation: One
Power Plant: 1,600 hp BMW 801C-1 air-cooled radial
Dimensions: Span 10.5 m (34.45 ft); length 8.84 m (29 ft); wing area 18.3 m² (196.98 sq ft)
Weights: Empty 3,170 kg (7,000 lb); MTOW 4,900 kg (10,805 lb)
Performance: Maximum speed 654 km/h (408 mph) at 6,000 m (19,686 ft); operational ceiling 11,400 m (37,403 ft); range 805 km (500 miles)
Load: For 20 mm cannon and two 13 mm machine guns, plus up to 1,000 kg (2,205 lb) of bombs

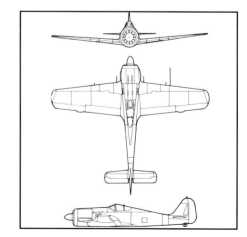

Focke-Wulf Fw 190A

LOCKHEED P-38 LIGHTNING (U.S.A.)

P-38J Lightning

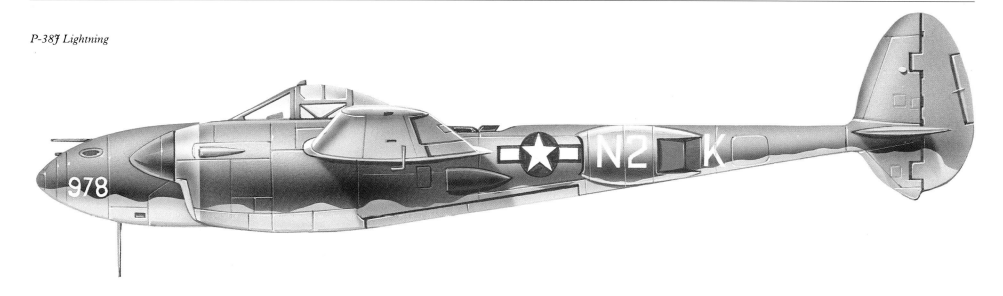

The Lightning was one was the more important fighters of World War II and, though it was not as nimble as a machine as single-engined types, found its métier in the long-range role with heavy armament and high performance. The machine resulted from a 1937 specification issued by the U.S. Army Air Corps for a high-performance fighter providing such speed, climb rate and range that a single-engined aircraft was virtually out of the question. Having opted for the twin-engined configuration, the design team then chose an unconventional layout with a central nacelle and twin booms extending as rearward extensions of the engine nacelle to accommodate the turbochargers and support the wide-span tailplane and oval vertical surfaces.

The XP-38 prototype flew in January 1939 with 716-kW (960-hp) Allison V-1710-11/15 engines driving opposite-rotating propellers. Development was protracted, and the first of 30 P-38s, with V-1710-27/29 engines, did not enter service until late 1941. Production totalled 10,037 in variants that included 36 P-36Ds with a revised tail unit and self-sealing fuel tanks, 210 P-38Es with the nose armament revised from one 37-mm cannon and four 12.7-mm (0.5-in) machine guns to one 20-mm cannon and four machine guns, 527 P-38Fs for tropical service with V-1710 49/53 engines, 1,082 F-38Gs with V-1710-

55/55 engines and provision for 907-kg (2,000-lb) of underwing stores, 601 P-38Gs with 1062-kW (1,425-hp) V-1710-89/91s and greater underwing stores load, 2,970 P-38Js with an improved engine installation and greater fuel capacity, 3,810 P-38Ls with 1193-kW (1,600-hp) V-1710-111/113s, provision for underwing rockets and, in some aircraft, a revised nose accommodating radar or a bomb-aimer for use as a bomber leader, the P-38M conversions of P-38L as two-seat night fighters, and the F-4 and F-5 conversions.

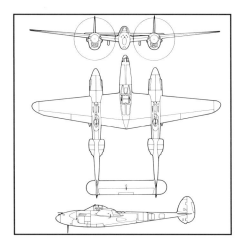

Lockheed P-38J Lightning

LOCKHEED P-38L LIGHTNING
Role: Long-range fighter bomber
Crew/Accommodation: One
Power Plant: Two 1,475 hp Allison V-1710-111 water-cooled inlines
Dimensions: Span 15.85 m (52 ft); length 11.53 m (37.83 ft); wing area 30.47 m² (327 sq ft)
Weights: Empty 5,806 kg (12,800 lb); MTOW 9,798 kg (21,600 lb)
Performance: Maximum speed 666 km/h (414 mph) at 7,620 m (25,000 ft); operational ceiling 13,410 m (44,000 ft); range 725 km (450 miles) with 1,451 kg (3,200 lb) of bombs
Load: One 20 mm cannon and four .5 inch machine guns, plus up to 1,451 kg (3,200 lb) of bombs

Lockheed P-38L Lightning

MITSUBISHI A6M REISEN 'ZEKE' (Japan)

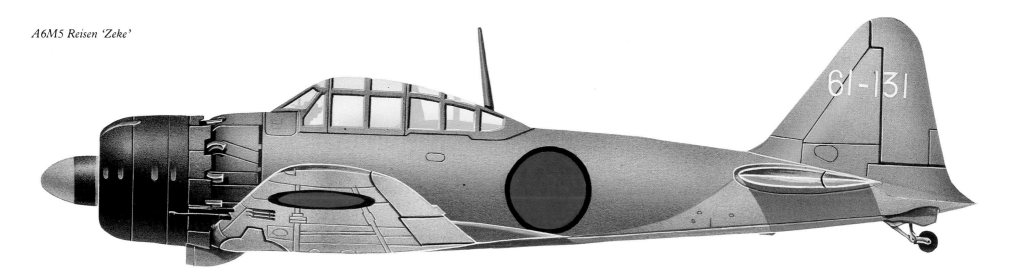

A6M5 Reisen 'Zeke'

The A6M Reisen (Zero Fighter) will rightly remain Japan's best known aircraft of World War II, and was in its early days, without doubt, the finest carrierborne fighter anywhere in the world. The A6M was the first naval fighter able to deal on equal terms with the best of land-based fighters, and was notable for its heavy firepower combined with good performance, great range and considerable agility. This combination could only be achieved with a lightweight and virtually unprotected airframe. Thus from 1943 the Zero

could not be developed effectively to maintain it as a competitive fighter.

The A6M was planned to an Imperial Japanese Navy Air Force requirement for a successor to the Mitsubishi A5M, a low-wing fighter with an open cockpit and fixed landing gear. The first of two A6M1 prototypes flew in April 1939 with a 582-kW (780-hp) Mitsubishi Mk2 Zuisei radial. The new fighter was a cantilever low-wing monoplane with retractable tailwheel landing gear, an enclosed cockpit and powerful armament. Performance and agility

were generally excellent, but the type was somewhat slower than anticipated. The sole A6M2 prototype therefore introduced the 690-kW (925-hp) Nakajima NK1C Sakae radial, and this was retained for the first series-built A6M2 aircraft that entered service with the designation Navy Type 0 Carrier Fighter Model 11. Production of the series amounted to 11,283 aircraft to the end of World War II, and major variants after the A6M2 were the A6M3 with the 843-kW (1,130-hp) Sakae 21 and clipped wingtips, the A6M5 with improved

armament and armour in three subvariants, the A6M6 with the Sakae 31, and the A6M7 dive-bomber and fighter. There were also a number of experimental and development models as well as the A6M2-N floatplane fighter built by Nakajima. The principal Allied reporting name for the type was 'Zeke'.

A Mitsubishi A6M5 Reisen

MITSUBISHI A6M5 'ZEKE'
Role: Naval carrierborne fighter
Crew/Accommodation: One
Power Plant: One 1,130 hp Nakajima Sakae 21 air-cooled radial
Dimensions: Span 11 m (36.09 ft); length 9.09 m (29.82 ft); wing area 21.3 m² (229.3 sq ft)
Weights: Empty 1,894 kg (4,176 lb) MTOW 2,952 kg (6,508 lb)
Performance: Maximum speed 565 km/h (351 mph) at 6,000 m (19,685 ft); operational ceiling 11,740 m (38,517 ft); range 1,570 km (976 miles)
Load: Two 20 mm cannon and two 7.7 mm machine guns

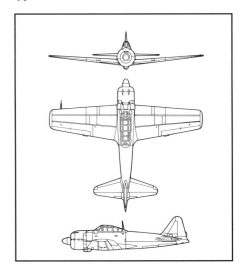

Mitsubishi A6M3 32 Reisen

BELL P-39 AIRACOBRA (U.S.A.)

P-39 Airacobra Mk I

The P-39 Airacobra was an attempt to create a fighter that possessed greater manoeuvrability and more powerful nose-mounted armament than contemporary fighters. The engine was located behind the cockpit on the aircraft's centre of gravity. It drove the propeller by means of an extension shaft, and the nose volume was left free for the forward unit of the retractable tricycle landing gear and also for heavy fixed armament including one 37-mm cannon firing through the propeller shaft. The XP-39 prototype flew in April 1938, and was followed by 13 YP-39 pre-production aircraft including one YP-39A with an unturbocharged Allison V-1710 engine. This last became the prototype for the production version, which was ordered in August 1939 as the P-45. These aircraft were in fact delivered as 20 P-39Cs and 60 P-39Ds with heavier armament and self-sealing tanks. Large-scale production followed. Total P-39 production was 9,590, even though the Airacobra was never more than adequate as a fighter and found its real mileu in the low-level attack role.

The main models were the 229 P-39Fs modelled on the P-39D but with an Aeroproducts propeller, the 210 P-39Ks with the V-1710-63 engine and a Curtiss propeller, 240 P-39Ms with the V-1710-83 engine and a larger propeller, 2,095 P-39Ns with the V-1710-85 engine but less fuel and armour, and 4,905 P-39Qs with two underwing gun gondolas. Large numbers were supplied to the U.S.S.R. in World War II.

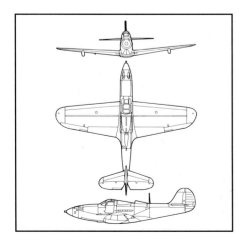

BELL P-39D AIRACOBRA
Role: Fighter
Crew/Accommodation: One
Power Plant: One, 1,150 hp Allison V-1710-35 water-cooled inline
Dimensions: Span 10.36 m (34 ft); length 9.19 m (30.16 ft); wing area 19.79 m² (213 sq ft)
Weights: Empty 2,478 kg (5,462 lb); MTOW 3,720 kg (8,200 lb)
Performance: Maximum speed 592 km/h (368 mph) at 4,206 m (13,800 ft); operational ceiling 9,784 m (32,100 ft); range 1,287 km (800 miles) with 227 kg (500 lb) of bombs
Load: One 37mm cannon, plus two .5 inch and four .303 inch machine guns, along with 227 kg (500 lb) of bombs

P-39N of the Italian Air Force

MIKOYAN-GUREVICH MiG-1 and MiG-3 (U.S.S.R.)

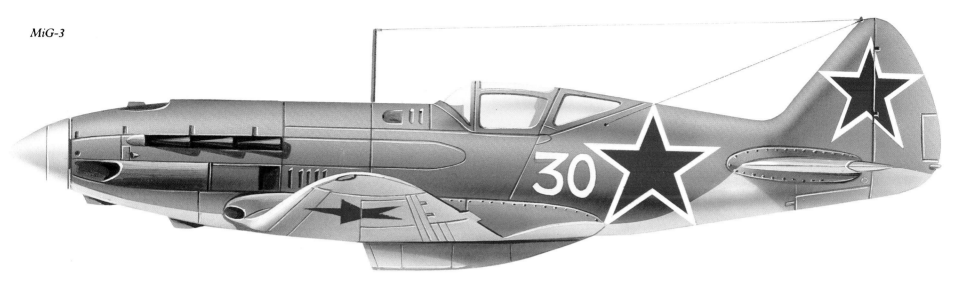

MiG-3

To design the new interceptor fighter requested by the Soviet Air Force in 1938, Artem Mikoyan and Mikhail Gurevich started a collaboration that led eventually to a succession of world-famous fighters. The two men's first effort was not so successful. As the starting point for the new interceptor, the MiG team produced I-65 and I-61 design concepts, the latter in variants with the Mikulin AM-35A and AM-37 inlines. The I-61 was deemed superior and ordered in the form of three I-200 prototypes.

The first of these flew in April 1940, and on the power of the AM-35A the type proved to have the excellent speed of 630 km/h (391 mph), making it the world's fastest interceptor of the period. The type was ordered into production as the MiG-1 with an open cockpit or a side-hinged canopy, and an armament of one 12.7-mm (0.5-in) and two 7.62-mm (0.3-in) machine guns. But range and longitudinal stability were both minimal, and structural integrity was inadequate after battle damage had been suffered, so only 100 were delivered before the MiG-1 was superseded by the strengthened and aerodynamically refined MiG-3. This had a rearward-sliding canopy, increased dihedral on the outer wing panels, greater fuel capacity, better armour protection and provision for weightier armament in the form of 200-kg (440-lb) of bombs or six 82-mm (3.2-in) rockets carried under the wings. Some 3,322 such aircraft were built, but these saw only limited use; the MiG-3 performed well at altitudes over 5000 m (16,405 ft), but most air combats with the generally better flown German fighters of the period took place at the low and medium altitudes below this height.

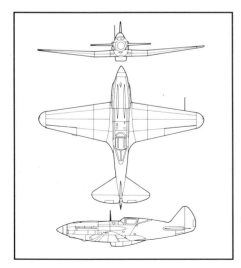

Mikoyan-Gurevich MiG-3

MIKOYAN-GUREVICH MiG-3
Role: Fighter
Crew/Accommodation: One
Power Plant: One 1,350 hp Mikulin AM-35A water-cooled inline
Dimensions: Span 10.3 m (33.79 ft); length 8.15 m (26.74 ft); wing area 17.44 m² (187.7 sq ft)
Weights: Empty 2,595 kg (5,720 lb); MTOW 3,285 kg (7,242 lb)
Performance: Maximum speed 640 km/h (398 mph) at 7,000 m (22,965 ft); operational ceiling 12,000 m (39,370 ft) range 820 km/h (510 miles) with full warload
Load: Three 12.7 mm machine guns, plus up to 200 kg (441 lb) of bombs or rockets

Mikoyan-Gurevich MiG-3

VOUGHT F4U CORSAIR (U.S.A.)

A-7P Corsair II

One of several fighters with a realistic claim to having been the best fighter of World War II, the Corsair was certainly the war's best fighter-bomber and a truly distinguished type in this exacting role with cannon, bombs and rockets. The type originated as the V.166A design in response to a U.S. Navy requirement of 1938 for a high-performance carrierborne fighter. The

design team produced the smallest possible airframe round the most powerful engine available, the 1491-kW (2,000-hp) Pratt & Whitney XR-2800 Double Wasp radial. This engine required a large-diameter propeller, and to provide this with adequate ground clearance without recourse to stalky main landing gear legs, the design team opted for inverted gull wings that allowed short main gear legs and also helped to keep the type's height as low as possible with the wings folded.

The V.166B prototype first flew in May 1940 as the XF4U-1, and after a troubled development in which the U.S. Navy refused to allow carrierborne operations until after the British had achieved these on their smaller carriers, the type entered service as the F4U-1. Total production was 12,571 up to the early 1950s, and the main variants were the baseline F4U-1 (758 aircraft), the F4U-1A (2,066) with a frameless canopy, the F4U-1C (200) with four 20-mm cannon in place of the wing

machine-guns, the F4U-1D (1,375) fighter-bomber, the F4U-1P photo-reconnaissance conversion of the F4U-1, the FG-1 built by Goodyear in three subvariants (1,704 FG-1s, 2,302 FG-1Ds and FG-1E night fighters in the FG-1 total), the F3A built by Brewster in two subvariants (735 F3A-1s and F3A-1Ds), the F4U-4 (2,351) with the 1827-kW (2,450-hp) R-2800-18W(C), a few of the F25 Goodyear version of the F4U-4, and several F4U-5, F4U-7 and AU-1 post-war models.

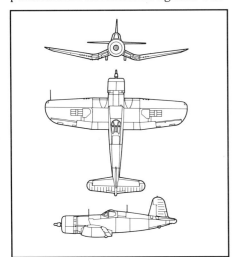

Vought F4U-1D Corsair

VOUGHT F4U-1D CORSAIR
Role: Naval carrierborne fighter bomber
Crew/Accommodation: One
Power Plant: One 2,000 hp Pratt & Whitney R-2800-8 Double Wasp air-cooled radial
Dimensions: Span 12.50 m (41 ft); length 10.16 m (33.33 ft); wing area 29.17 m² (314 sq ft)
Weights: Empty 4,074 kg (8,982 lb); MTOW 6,350 kg (14,000 lb)
Performance: Maximum speed 578 km/h (359 mph) at sea level; operating ceiling 11,247 m (36,900 ft); range 1,633 km (1,015 miles)
Load: Six .5 inch machine guns plus up to 907 kg (2,000 lb) of bombs

A Vought AU-1 Corsair with the markings of the US Marine Corps

NORTH AMERICAN P-51 MUSTANG (U.S.A.)

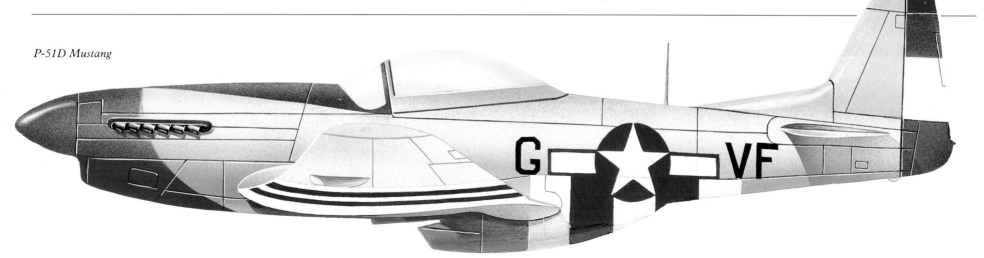

P-51D Mustang

The Mustang was perhaps the greatest fighter of World War II in terms of all-round performance and capability, and resulted from a British requirement of April 1940 that stipulated a first flight within 120 days of contract signature. The NA-73X flew in October of the same year with an 820-kW (1,100-hp) Allison V-1710-F3R inline. Mustang production totalled 15,469, and the first variant was the Mustang Mk I reconnaissance fighter with an armament of four 12.7-mm (0.5-in) machine-guns; two of these 620 aircraft were evaluated by

the U.S. Army Air Corps with the designation XP-51. The next variants were the 93 Mustang Mk IAs and 57 equivalent P-51s with four 20-mm cannon, and the 50 longer-range Mustang Mk IIs and 250 equivalent P-51As with more power and four machine-guns. U.S. Army offshoots were the F-6 and F-6A reconnaissance aircraft and the A-36A Apache dive-bomber and ground-attack aircraft.

Tactical capability was hampered by the V-1710 engine, so the basic airframe was revised to take the Rolls-Royce Merlin built under licence in

the United States by Packard as the V-1650. Production versions were the 910 Mustang Mk IIIs with four machine-guns and the equivalent P-51B and P-51C, respectively 1,988 and 1,750 aircraft with original and bubble canopies; there were also F-6C reconnaissance aircraft. The classic and most extensively built variant was the P-51D (7l,966, of which 875 became British Mustang Mk IVs) with a cutdown rear fuselage, a bubble canopy, six machine-guns, greater power and more fuel; the F-6D was the reconnaissance version. The P-51D had the range to escort U.S. bombers on deep raids, and was the decisive fighter of the second half of

World War II.

Later variants expanded on the theme of the P-51D: the 555 P-51Hs were of a lightened version, the 1,337 P-51Ks were of a similarly lightened variant with an Aeroproducts propeller, and the F-6K was the reconnaissance conversion of the P-51K. The type was also built under licence in Australia with designations running from Mustang Mk 20 to Mustang Mk 24.

North American P-51D Mustang

NORTH AMERICAN P-51D MUSTANG
Role: Day fighter
Crew/Accommodation: One
Power Plant: One 1,450 hp Packard/Rolls Royce Merlin V-1650-7 water-cooled inline
Dimensions: Span 11.28 m (37 ft); length 9.83 m (32.25 ft); wing area 21.83 m² (235 sq ft)
Weights: Empty 3,466 kg (7,635 lb); MTOW 5,493 kg (12,100 lb)
Performance: Maximum speed 703 km/h (437 mph) at 7,625 m (25,000 ft); operational ceiling 12,192 m (40,000 ft); range 2,655 km (1,650 miles) with maximum fuel
Load: Six .5 inch machine guns, plus up to 907 kg (2,000 lb) of externally carried bombs or fuel tanks

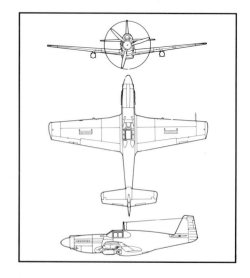

North American A-36A Apache

REPUBLIC P-47 THUNDERBOLT

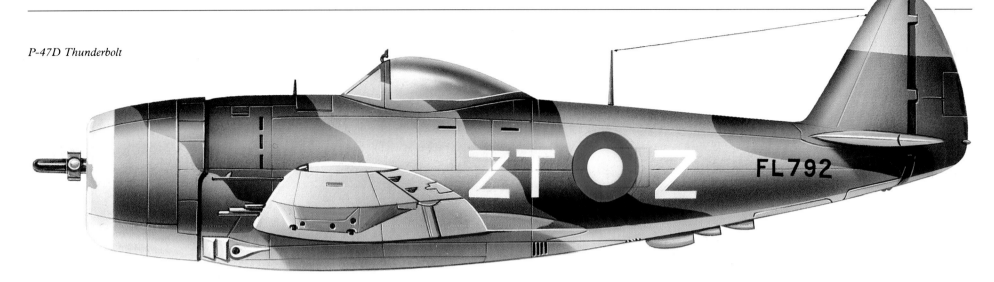

P-47D Thunderbolt

The Thunderbolt was one of a trio of superb American fighters to see extensive service in World War II. The massive fuselage of this heavyweight fighter was dictated by the use of a large turbocharger, which was located in the rear fuselage for balance reasons and therefore had to be connected to the engine by extensive lengths of wide-diameter ducting. The type was clearly related to Republic's early portly-fuselage fighters, the P-35 and P-43 Lancer, but was marked by very high performance, high firepower and great structural strength.

The XP-47B prototype flew in May 1941 with the 1380-kW (1,850-hp) XR-2800 radial, later revised to develop 1491 kW (2,000 hp). This formed the basis of the 171 P-47B production aircraft with the R-2800-21 radial, and the 602 P-47Cs with a longer forward fuselage for the same engine or, in later examples, the 1715-kW (2,300-hp) R-2800-59 radial; the type also featured provision for a drop tank or bombs. The P-47D was the main production model, 12,602 being built with the 1715-kW (2,300 hp) R-2800-21W or 1890-kW (2,535-hp) R-2800-59W water-injected radials, as well as a greater load of external stores that could include 1134-kg (2,500-lb) of bombs or ten 127-mm (5-in) rockets in the fighter-bomber role that became an increasingly important part of the Thunderbolt's repertoire. Early aircraft had the original 'razorback' canopy/rear fuselage, but later machines introduced a 360° vision bubble canopy and a cutdown rear fuselage. P-47G was the designation given to 354 Wright-built P-47Ds. and the only other production models were the 130 P-47M 'sprinters' with the 2088-kW (2,800-hp) R-2800-57(C) radial and the 1,816 P-47N long-range aircraft with a strengthened and longer wing plus the 2088-kW (2,800-hp) R-2800-77 radial. The Thunderbolt was never an effective close-in fighter, but excelled in the high-speed dive-and-zoom attacks useful in long-range escort.

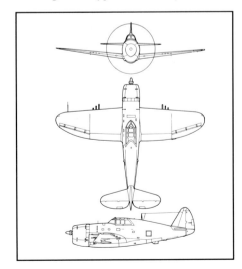

Republic P-47C Thunderbolt

REPUBLIC P-47C THUNDERBOLT
Role: Fighter
Crew/Accommodation: One
Power Plant: One 2,000 hp Pratt & Whitney R-2800-21 Double Wasp air-cooled radial
Dimensions: Span 12.42 m (40.75 ft); length 10.99 m (36,08 ft); wing area 27.87 m² (300 sq ft)
Weights: Empty 4,491 kg (9,900 lb); MTOW 6,770 kg (14,925 lb)
Performance: Maximum speed 697 km/h (433 mph) at 9,144 m (30,000 ft); operational ceiling 12,802 m (42,000 ft); range 722 km (480 miles) with a 227 kg (500 lb) bomb
Load: Eight .5 inch machine guns, plus up to 227 kg (500 lb) of bombs

The Republic P-47D Thunderbolt

YAKOVLEV Yak-9 (U.S.S.R.)

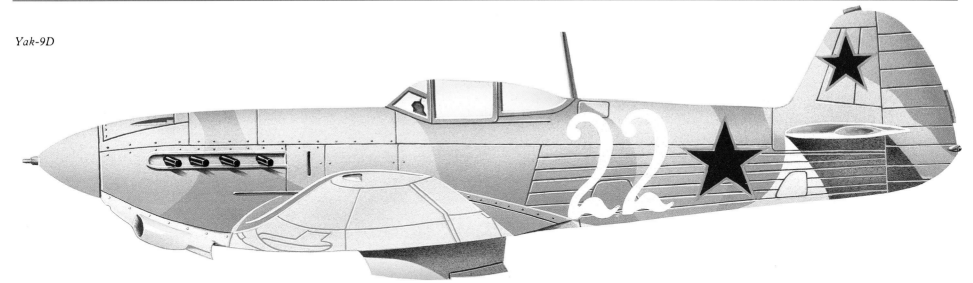

Yak-9D

The Yak-9 was one of the finest fighters of World War II, and was the most prolific culmination of the evolutionary design philosophy that started with the Yak-1. The Yak-9 entered combat during the Battle of Stalingrad late in 1942, and was a development of the Yak-7DI that was notable for its mixed wood and metal primary structure.

Production lasted to 1946 and totalled 16,769 aircraft in several important and some lesser variants. These included the original Yak-9 with the 969-kW (1,300-hp) Klimov VK-105PF-1 or 1014-kW (1,360-hp) VK-105PF-3 inline engine plus an armament of one 20-mm cannon and one or two 12.7-mm (0.5-in) machine guns, the Yak-9M with revised armament, the Yak-9D long-range escort fighter with the VK-105PF-3 engine and greater fuel capacity, the Yak-9T anti-tank variant with one 37- or 45-mm cannon and provision for anti-tank bomblets under the wings, the Yak-9K heavy anti-tank fighter with a 45-mm cannon in the nose, the Yak-9B high-speed light bomber with provision for four 100-kg (220-lb) bombs carried internally as part of a 600-kg (1,323-lb) total internal and external warload, the Yak-9MPVO night fighter carrying searchlights for the illumination of its quarry, the Yak-9DD very long-range escort fighter based on the Yak-9D but fitted for drop tanks, the Yak-9U conversion trainer in three subvariants, the YAK-9P post-war interceptor with the 1230-kW (1,650-hp) Klimov VK-107A inline and two fuselage-mounted 20-mm cannon, and the Yak-9R reconnaissance aircraft.

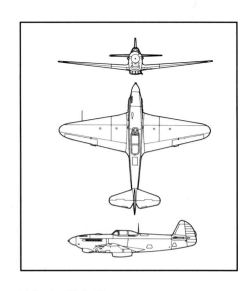

Yakovlev Yak-9D

YAKOVLEV Yak-9D
Role: Fighter
Crew/Accommodation: One
Power Plant: One 1,360 hp Klimov VK-105PF-3
Dimensions: Span 9.74 m (32.03 ft); length 8.55 m (28.05 ft); wing area 17.1 m² (184.05 sq ft)
Weights: Empty 2,770 kg (6,107 lb); MTOW 3,080 kg (6,790 lb)
Performance: Maximum speed 602 km/h (374 mph) at 2,000 m (6,560 ft); operational ceiling 10,600 m (34,775 ft); range 1,410 km (876 miles)
Load: One 20 mm cannon + one 12.7 mm machine gun

Yakovlev Yak-9DD long-range fighters

KAWASAKI Ki-61 HIEN and Ki-100 'TONY' (Japan)

Ki-61-I-KAIc Hién 'Tong'

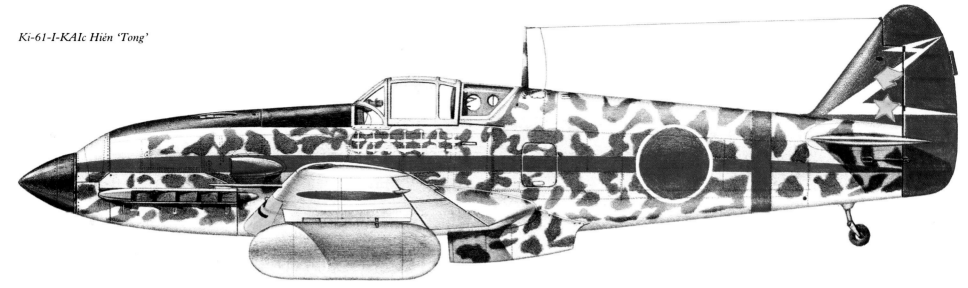

The Ki-61 Hien (Swallow) was the only inline-engined Japanese fighter to see substantial use in World War II, and was developed in parallel with the unsuccessful Ki-60 though using the same Kawasaki Ha-40 engine, a licence-built version of the Daimler-Benz DB 601A. The first Ki-61 prototype flew in December 1941. The Ki-61-I entered combat in April 1943 and soon acquired the Allied reporting name 'Tony'. By the time production ended in January 1945, 2,666 aircraft had been built in variants such as the Ki-61-I with two

7.7-mm (0.303-in) fuselage and two 12.7-mm (0.5-in) wing machine guns, the Ki-61-Ia with two 20-mm wing cannon, the Ki-61-Ib with 12.7-mm (0.5-in) fuselage machine guns, the Ki-61-Ic with a rationalized structure, and the Ki-61-Id with 30-mm wing cannon.

The Ki-61-II had a larger wing and the more powerful Ha-140 engine, but was so delayed in development that only 99 had been produced before United States Air Force bombing destroyed engine production capacity. Variants were the Ki-61-II KAI with

the Ki-61-I's wing, the Ki-61-IIa with the Ki-61-Ic's armament, and the Ki-61-IIb with four 20-mm wing cannon. With the Ha-140 engine unavailable for a comparatively large number of completed Ki-61-II airframes, the Japanese army ordered the type adapted to take the Mitsubishi Ha-112-II radial engine, the 1119-kW (1,500-hp) rating of which was identical to that of the Ha-140. The resulting Ki-100 first flew in 1945 and proved an outstanding interceptor, perhaps Japan's best fighter of World War II, also known to the Allies as 'Tony'. The army ordered completion

of the 272 Ki-61-II airframes as Ki-100-Ia fighters, while new production amounted to 99 Ki-100-Ib aircraft with the cut-down rear fuselage and bubble canopy developed for the proposed Ki-61-III fighter. The designation Ki-100-II was used for three prototypes with the Mitsubishi Ha-112-IIru turbocharged radial for improved high-altitude performance.

This is a Ki-61-I.

KAWASAKI KI-100-II 'TONY'
Role: Fighter
Crew/Accommodation: One
Power Plant: One 1,500 hp Mitsubishi Ha-112-II air-cooled radial
Dimensions: Span 12 m (39.37 ft); length 8.82 m (28.94 ft); wing area 20 m² (215.3 sq ft)
Weights: Empty 2,522 kg (5,567 lb); MTOW 3,495 kg (7,705 lb)
Performance: Maximum speed 590 km/h (367 mph) at 10,000 m (32,808 ft); operational ceiling 11,500 m (37,500 ft); range 1,800 km (1,118 miles)
Load: Two 20 mm cannon and two 12.7 mm machine guns

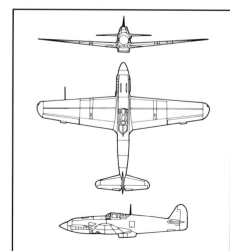

Kawasaki Ki-61 KAIc

FAIREY FIREFLY (United Kingdom)

Firefly AS.Mk 6

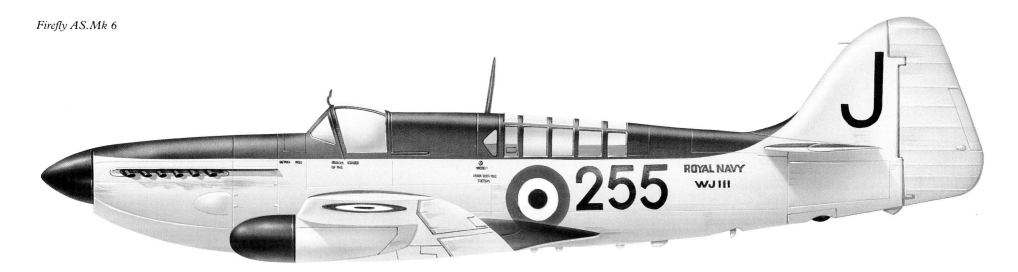

Designed to a requirement for a carrierborne two-seat reconnaissance fighter and first flown in December 1941 as the first of four prototypes powered by the 1290-kW (1,730-hp) Rolls-Royce Griffon IIB inline engine, the Firefly was one of the Royal Navy's most successful warplanes of the 1940s. The type had an all-metal construction, low-set cantilever wings, retractable tailwheel landing gear, and naval features like folding wings and an arrester hook.

The Firefly Mk I initial production series featured wings spanning 13.55 m (44 ft 6 in) and the 1484-kW (1,990-hp) Rolls-Royce Griffon XII with a chin radiator, and was produced in F.Mk I fighter, FR.Mk I fighter reconnaissance, NF.Mk I night-fighter and T.Mk I trainer versions to the extent of 937 aircraft. The 37 Firefly NF.Mk II night fighters had a longer nose and different radar, but were soon converted to Mk I standard.

Post-war conversions of the Mk I were the Firefly T.Mk 1 pilot trainer, T.Mk 2 operational trainer, and T.Mk 3 anti-submarine warfare trainer. The Firefly Mk IV switched to the 1566-kW (2,100-hp) Griffon 61 with root radiators in wings spanning 12.55 m (41 ft 2 in), and was produced in F.Mk IV and FR.Mk 4 versions. The Firefly Mk 5 introduced power-folding wings, and was produced in FR.Mk 5, NF.Mk 5, T.Mk 5 and anti-submarine AS.Mk 5 versions. The AS.Mk 6 was identical to the AS.Mk 5 other than in its use of British rather than American sonobuoys. The last production model, which raised the overall construction total to 1,623 aircraft, was the Firefly AS.Mk 7, which had the original long-span wing and a 1678-kW (2,250-hp) Griffon 59 with a chin radiator. Surplus Fireflies were also converted as remotely controlled target drones for the British surface-to-air missile programme.

The Fairey Firefly FR.Mk 5 was a two-seat reconnaissance fighter

FAIREY FIREFLY FR. Mk 5
Role: Fighter reconnaissance
Crew/Accommodation: Two
Power Plant: One 2,250 hp Rolls-Royce Griffon 74 water-cooled inline
Dimensions: Span 12.55 m (41.17 ft); length 11.56 m (37.91 ft); wing area 30.65 m² (330 sq ft)
Weights: Empty 4,389 kg (9,674 lb); MTOW 6,114 kg (13,479 lb)
Performance: Maximum speed 618 km/h (386 mph) at 4,270 m (14,000 ft); operational ceiling 8,660m (28,400 ft); range 2,090 km (1,300 miles) with long-range tankage
Load: Four 20 mm cannon, plus up to 454 kg (1,000 lb) of externally underslung bombs

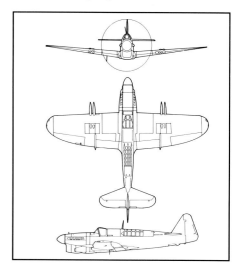

Fairey Firefly F.Mk I

GRUMMAN F6F HELLCAT (U.S.A.)

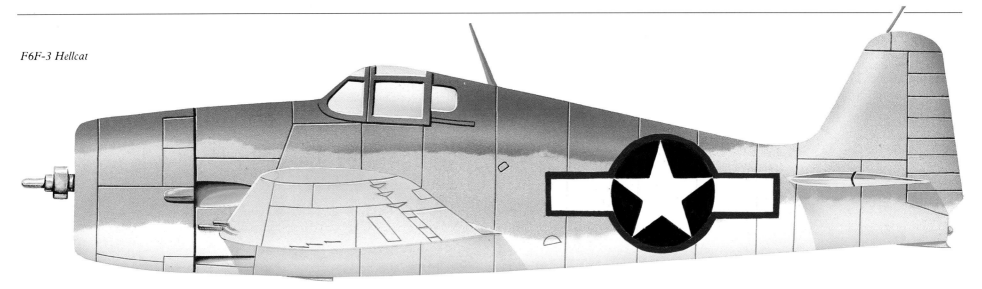

F6F-3 Hellcat

The Hellcat was the logical successor to the Wildcat with more size and power in a generally similar airframe with a low- rather than mid-set wing. A number of operational improvements suggested by Wildcat experience were incorporated in the basic design, and after evaluating this, the U.S. Navy contracted in June 1941 for a total of four XF6F prototypes. These were built with different Wright and Pratt & Whitney engine installations (normally aspirated and turbocharged R-2600 Cyclone and R-2800 Double Wasp units respectively). In June 1942, the

XF6F-1 became the first of these to fly, and the type selected for production was the XF6F-3 powered by the 1491-kW (2,000-hp) R-2800-10 Double Wasp with a two-stage turbocharger. This model entered production as the F6F-3 and reached squadrons in January 1944; the Fleet Air Arm designated the type Gannet Mk I, but later changed the name to Hellcat Mk I. Production lasted to mid-1944, and amounted to 4,423 aircraft including 18 F6F-3E and 205 F6F-3N night fighters with different radar equipments in pods under their starboard wings.

That the Hellcat was in all significant respects 'right' is attested by the relatively few variants emanating from a large production run that saw the delivery of 12,275 aircraft in all. From early 1944, production switched to the F6F-5 (Hellcat Mk II) with aerodynamic refinements including a revised cowling, new ailerons, a strengthened tail unit, and the R-2800-10W radial the suffix of which indicated the water injection system that produced a 10 per cent power boost for take-off and combat. These 6,436 aircraft also

featured provision for underwing bombs or rockets. There were also 1,189 examples of the F6F-5N (Hellcat NF.Mk II) night fighter, and some F6F-5 and F6F-5N fighters were also converted as F6F-5P photo-reconnaissance aircraft. Hellcat pilots claimed 4,947 aircraft shot down in combat, more than 75 per cent of all 'kills' attributed to U.S. Navy pilots in World War II.

A pair of F6F-5 fighter-bombers

GRUMMAN F6F-5 HELLCAT
Role: Naval carrierborne fighter
Crew/Accommodation: One
Power Plant: One 2,000 hp Pratt & Whitney R-2800-10W Double Wasp air-cooled radial
Dimensions: Span 13.06 m (42.83 ft); length 10.31 m (33.83 ft); wing area 31.03 m² (334 sq ft)
Weights: Empty 4,100 kg (9,060 lb); MTOW 5,714 kg (12,598 lb)
Performance: Maximum speed 612 km/h (380 mph) at 7,132 m (23,400 ft); operational ceiling 11,369 m (37,300 ft); range 1,521 km (945 miles)
Load: Two 20 mm cannon and four .5 inch machine guns, plus up to 975 kg (2,150 lb) of weapons, including one torpedo

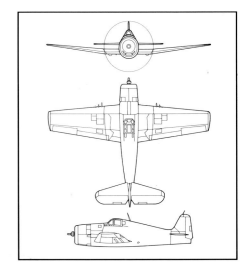

Grumman F6F-3 Hellcat

HAWKER TEMPEST (United Kingdom)

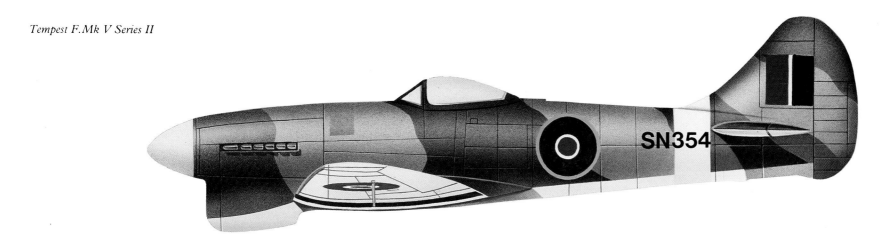

Tempest F.Mk V Series II

The failure of the Hawker Typhoon in its designed interceptor role left the British short of an advanced interceptor; in 1941 it was suggested the Typhoon be revised with a thinner, elliptical wing with low-drag radiators in the leading edges to replace the Typhoon's chin radiator. In November 1941 two prototypes were ordered with the Napier Sabre inline. Early in 1942, the type was renamed Tempest. The two original prototypes became the Tempest F.Mks I and V with the Sabre IV and II respectively, and another four prototypes were ordered as two Tempest F.Mk IIs with the 1879-kW (2,520-hp) Bristol Centaurus radial and two Tempest F.Mk IIIs with the Rolls-Royce Griffon IIB inline, the latter becoming Tempest F.Mk IVs when fitted with the Griffon 61.

Initial orders were placed for 400 Tempest F.Mk Is, and the first such fighter flew in February 1943. The engine suffered development problems, however, and the variant was abandoned. The first Tempest to fly had been the Tempest F.Mk V in September 1942, and an eventual 800 were built as 100 Tempest F.Mk V Series I and 700 Series II aircraft with long- and short-barrel cannon respectively, some later being converted as Tempest TT.Mk 5 target tugs. The Tempest Mk II materialized with the Centaurus V radial, and production for post-war service amounted to 136 F.Mk II fighters and 338 FB.Mk II fighter-bombers. The only other production model was the Tempest F.Mk VI, of which 142 were produced for tropical service with the 1745-kW (2,340-hp) Sabre V. Some of these were later adapted as Tempest TT.Mk 6s.

Tempest F.Mk V

HAWKER TEMPEST Mk V
Role: Stike fighter
Crew/Accommodation: One
Power Plant: One 2,180 hp Napier Sabre IIA water-cooled inline
Dimensions: Span 12.49 m (41 ft); length 10.26 m (33.67 ft); wing area 28.05 m² (302 sq ft)
Weights: Empty 4,196 kg (9,250 lb); MTOW 6,187 kg (13,640 lb)
Performance: Maximum speed 700 km/h (435 mph) at 5,180 m (17,000 ft); operational ceiling 11,125 m (36,500 ft); range 1,191 km (740 miles) on internal fuel only
Load: Four 20 mm cannon, plus up to 907 kg (2,000 lb) of bombs or rockets

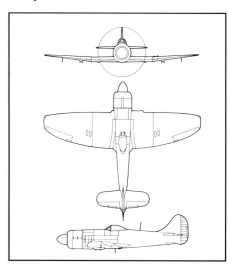

Hawker Tempest F.Mk II

DORNIER Do 335 PFEIL (Germany)

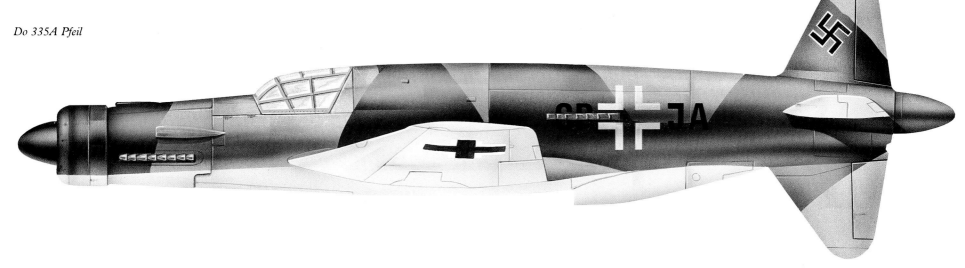

Do 335A Pfeil

The unusual configuration of the Do 335 Pfeil (Arrow) was designed to allow the installation of two powerful engines in a minimum-drag layout that would also present no single-engined asymmetric thrust problems. Dr Claudius Dornier patented the concept in 1937, and the configuration was successfully evaluated in the Göppingen Gö 9 research aircraft during 1939. Dornier then developed the basic concept as a high-performance fighter, but the Do P.231 type was adopted by the Reichsluftfahrtministerium (German Air Ministry) as a high-speed bomber. Initial work had reached an advanced stage when the complete project was cancelled. There then emerged a German need for a high-performance interceptor, and the wheel turned full circle as Dornier was instructed to revive its design in this role.

The resulting aircraft was of all-metal construction, and in layout was a low-wing monoplane with sturdy retractable tricycle landing gear, cruciform tail surfaces, and two 1342-kW (1,800-hp) Daimler-Benz DB 603 inline engines each driving a three-blade propeller. One engine was mounted in the conventional nose position, and the other in the rear fuselage powering a propeller aft of the tail unit by means of an extension shaft. The first of 14 prototypes flew in September 1943. Considerable development flying was undertaken by these one- and two-seater models, and 10 Do 335A-O pre-production fighter-bombers were evaluated from the late summer of 1944. The first production model was the Do 335A-1, of which 11 were completed. None of these entered full-scale service, though some were allocated to a service test unit in the spring of 1945. The only other aircraft completed were two examples of the Do 335A-12 two-seat trainer. There were also many projected variants.

Dornier Do 335A-O Pfeil

DORNIER Do 335A-O PFEIL
Role: Long range day fighter
Crew/Accommodation: One
Power Plant: Two 2,250 hp Daimler-Benz DB 603E/MW50 liquid-cooled inlines
Dimensions: Span 13.80 m (45.28 ft); length 13.85 m (45.44 ft); wing area 38.50 m² (414.41 sq ft)
Weights: Empty 7,400 kg (16,315 lb); MTOW 9,600 kg (21,160 lb)
Performance: Maximum speed 768 km/h (477 mph) at 6,890 m (21,000 ft); operational ceiling 11,400 m (37,400 ft); radius 1,397 km (868 miles) at military power
Load: One 30 mm and two 15 mm cannons, plus a 500 kg (1,103 lb) bomb

Dornier Do 335 Pfeil

KAWANISHI N1K 'REX' and 'GEORGE' (Japan)

N1K2-1 'George'

Designed from 1940 as a fighter able to protect and support amphibious landings, the N1K was schemed as a substantial seaplane with single main/ two stabilizing floats and a powerful engine driving contra-rotating propellers that would mitigate torque problems during take-off and landing. The first prototype flew in May 1942 with the 1089-kW (1,460-hp) Mitsubishi MK4D Kasei radial, but

problems with the contra-rotating propeller unit led to the use of a conventional propeller unit. The type began to enter service in 1943 as the N1K1 Kyofu (Mighty Wind), but the type's *raison d'être* had disappeared by this stage of the war and production was terminated with the 97th machine. The Allied reporting name for the N1K1 was 'Rex'.

The N1K2 with a more powerful engine remained only a project, but in 1942 the company began development of a landplane version as the N1K1-J Shiden (Violet Lightning) with

retractable tailwheel landing gear and the 1357-kW (1,820-hp) Nakajima NK9H Homare 11 radial. This suffered a number of teething problems, and its need for a large-diameter propeller dictated the design of telescoping main landing gear legs. The new type flew in prototype form during December 1942, but development difficulties delayed the type's service debut to early 1944. N1K1-J production totalled 1,007 in three subvariants known to the Allies

as the 'George'. Yet this had been planned as an interim version pending deliveries of the N1K2-J version with a low- rather than mid-set wing, a longer fuselage, a revised tail unit, and less complicated main landing gear units. Only 423 of this version were produced. The N1K3-J, N1K4-J and N1K5-J prototypes had a longer forward fuselage, the 1491-kW (2,000-hp) Homare 23 engine and the 1641-kW (2,200-hp) Mitsubishi MK9A radial engine respectively.

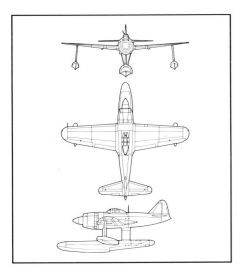

Kawanishi N1K1 'Rex'

KAWANISHI N1K1 'REX'
Role: Fighter floatplane
Crew/Accommodation: One
Power Plant: One 1,460 hp Mitsubishi Kasei 14 air-cooled radial
Dimensions: Span 12 m (39.37 ft); length 10.59 m (34.74 ft); wing area 23.5 m² (252.9 sq ft)
Weights: Empty 2,700 kg (5,952 lb); MTOW 3,712 kg (8,184 lb)
Performance: Maximum speed 482 km/h (300 mph) at 5,700 m (18,701 ft); operational ceiling 10,560 m (34,646 ft); range 1,690 km (1,050 miles) with full bombload
Load: Two 20 mm cannon, two 7.7 mm machine guns, plus up to 60 kg (132 lb) of bombs

The Kawanishi N1K2-J Shiden KAI.

de HAVILLAND D.H.103 HORNET (United Kingdom)

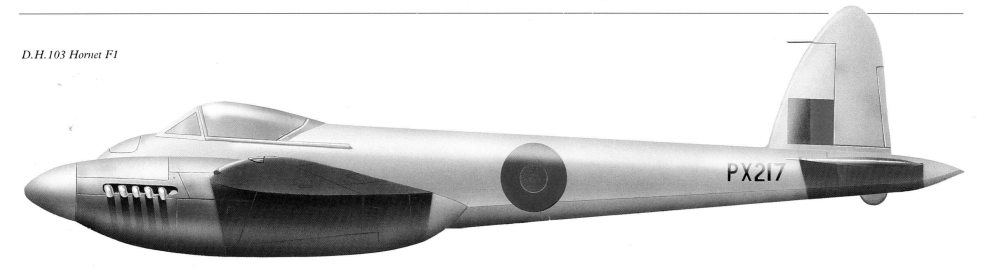

D.H.103 Hornet F1

The D.H.103 was designed to provide the British forces fighting the Japanese with a long-range fighter with the advantages of a twin-engined layout. The type was based on the aerodynamics of the Mosquito multi-role warplane, and so impressive were the estimated performance figures that a specification was written round the type in 1943. The D.H.103 retained the Mosquito's plywood/balsa/plywood structure for its single-seat fuselage, but featured new wood and metal wings. Work began in June 1943, and the first prototype flew in July 1944 with two Merlin 130/131 inline engines. Performance and handling were excellent, and initial deliveries were made in April 1945. This first model was the Hornet F.Mk 1, of which 60 were built, but it was too late for service in World War II.

The major variant of this land-based series was the Hornet F.Mk 3 with a dorsal fillet (retrofitted to earlier aircraft), greater internal fuel capacity, and provision for underwing loads of weapons or drop tanks. The last of 120 aircraft were delivered to Hornet FR.Mk 4 reconnaissance fighter standard with the rear fuselage fuel tank deleted to provide accommodation for a single camera. The basic design also appealed to the Fleet Air Arm, which ordered the navalized Sea Hornet series. Deliveries included 78 Sea Hornet F.Mk 20 fighters based on the F.Mk 3 and first flown in August 1946 for a final delivery in June 1951, 79 Sea Hornet NF.Mk 21 two-seat night fighters based on the F.Mk 20 but with radar in a revised nose, and 43 Sea Hornet PR.Mk 23 photo-reconnaissance aircraft based on the F.Mk 20 but with one night or two day cameras. The last Sea Hornets were retired in 1955.

Hornet F.Mk 3 of No.64 Squadron.

de HAVILLAND D.H.103 HORNET F.Mk 1
Role: Long range fighter
Crew/Accommodation: One
Power Plant: Two 2,070 hp Rolls-Royce Merlin 130/131 liquid-cooled inlines
Dimensions: Span 13.72 m (45.00 ft); length 11.18 m (36.66 ft); wing area 33.54 m² (361 sq ft)
Weights: Empty 5,671 kg (12,502) lb; MTOW 8,029 kg (17,700 lb)
Performance: Maximum speed 760 km/h (472 mph) at 6,706 m (22,000 ft); operational ceiling 11,430 m (37,500 ft); range 4,023 km (2,500 miles)
Load: Four 20 mm cannons

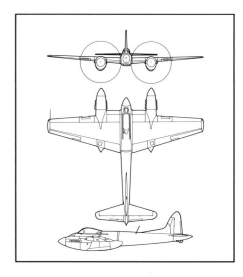

de Havilland Hornet F.Mk 3

HAWKER SEA FURY (United Kingdom)

Sea Fury FB.Mk 11

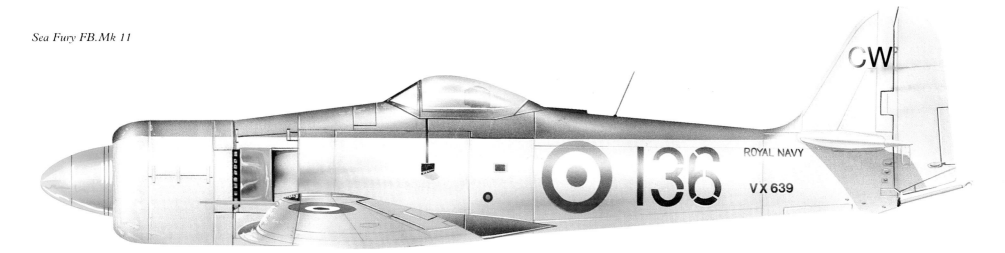

The origins of Hawker's second Fury fighter lay in a 1942 requirement for a smaller and lighter version of the Tempest, and was developed in parallel land-based and naval forms to 1943 specifications. Hawker was responsible for the overall design, with Boulton Paul allocated the task of converting the type for naval use. By December 1943, six prototypes had been ordered, one with the Bristol Centaurus XII radial, two with the Centaurus XXI radial, two with the Rolls-Royce Griffon inline, and one as a test airframe. The first to fly was a Centaurus XII-powered machine that took to the air in September 1944, followed in November by a Griffon-powered machine that was later re-engined with the Napier Sabre inline. Orders were placed for 200 land-based Fury and 100 carrierborne Sea Fury fighters, but the Fury order was cancelled at the end of World War II. The first Sea Fury flew in February 1945 with the Centaurus XII, and development continued after the war to produce the first fully navalized machine with folding wings and the Centaurus XV. This flew in October 1945, and paved the way for the Sea Fury F.Mk X, of which 50 were built.

The first type to enter widespread service was the Sea Fury FB.Mk 11 of which 615 were built including 31 and 35 for the Royal Australian and Royal Canadian Navies respectively. The Fleet Air Arm also took 60 Sea Fury T.Mk 20 trainers, of which 10 were later converted as target tugs for West Germany. Additional operators of new-build aircraft were the Netherlands with 22 Sea Fury F.Mk 50s and FB.Mk 50s, and Pakistan with 93 Sea Fury FB.Mk 60s and five T.Mk 61s. Other buyers were Burma (21 ex-British aircraft), Cuba (17 aircraft) and Iraq (60 aircraft).

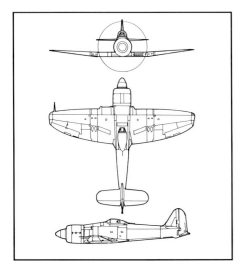

Hawker Sea Fury FB.Mk 11

HAWKER SEA FURY FB.Mk 11
Role: Carrierborne fighter bomber
Crew/Accommodation: One
Power Plant: One 2,480 hp Bristol Centaurus 18 air-cooled radial
Dimensions: Span 11.70 m (38.40 ft); length 10.57 m (34.67 ft); wing area 26.01 m² (280.00 sq ft)
Weights: Empty 4,191 kg (9,240 lb); MTOW 5,670 kg (12,500 lb)
Performance: Maximum speed 740 km/h (460 mph) at 5,486 m (18,000 ft); operational ceiling 10,912 m (35,800 ft); radius 1,127 km (700 miles) without external fuel tanks
Load: Four 20 mm cannons, plus up to 907 kg (2,000 lb) of bombs or twelve 3 inch rocket projectiles

The Hawker Sea Fury FB.Mk 11.

INDEX